TWIN LIGHTS
— *Tonic* —

TWIN LIGHTS

Tonic

CAPE ANN'S TIMELESS SODA POP

PAUL ST. GERMAIN AND DEVLIN SHERLOCK

THE
History
PRESS

Published by The History Press
Charleston, SC
www.historypress.com

Front cover: Artwork "Twin Lights Trio" © 2020 David Arsenault. Oil on canvas, private collection.
Back cover: Aerial photo of Thacher Island by Vincent Nappa; *inset*: bottle-washing machine from Pierce Sears collection.

First published 2021

Manufactured in the United States

ISBN 9781467148788

Library of Congress Control Number: 2020951672

Notice: The information in this book is true and complete to the best of our knowledge. It is offered without guarantee on the part of the authors or The History Press. The authors and The History Press disclaim all liability in connection with the use of this book.

CONTENTS

FOREWORD

Twin Lights "Tonic" has been an important part of the fabric of the community of Rockport, Massachusetts, for over 114 years, deeply woven into this small seaside community of artists, tourists and fishermen.

Pierce Sears, a lifelong resident of eighty-eight years, has continued to produce some of the best-tasting old-school "tonic," even though distribution has been reduced in recent years to special events in town like our annual Harvest Festival or special requests for birthdays. It seems everyone in town has a fond memory of partaking at a middle school dance, getting their favorite flavor at the loved Jimmy's at Front Beach or looking for bottles to redeem to buy penny candy at the country store. Pierce is a beloved individual who was willing to keep the machines working long enough so that our grandchildren—and, in some cases, great-grandchildren—can experience a moment in time when Twin Lights was as much a part of Rockport as visiting Motif Number 1 (our iconic red fish shack, painted and photographed by millions over the years). When I first met Pierce twenty years ago, having moved back to the North Shore and settled onto Bearskin Neck, Twin Lights was still being sold in a handful of local stores and at our Little Arts Cinema. I'll never forget attending a special showing of *Cinema Paradiso* and sipping a seven-ounce bottle of Twin Lights birch beer with my popcorn. The experience was a Norman Rockwell moment that will stay with me for the rest of my life!

Pierce and I became fast friends, bonding over our mutual love for old-time radio, professional wrestling and classic movies. We've attended monthly Old Time Radio Club meetings together for over a decade; traveled to classic film festivals from Syracuse, New York, to Hollywood, California; and even met a few professional wrestlers (including the late George "The Animal" Steele).

Additionally, I've served as curator for his vast eight-millimeter film collection. (Pierce began shooting film in the 1950s and continued doing so until the great blizzard of 1978.) We have enjoyed many nights viewing these films at his home and recording narrations for the many hours of Rockport and Gloucester footage that has been screened over the years at community events—where Twin Lights Tonic was also served, of course! We've also reproduced numerous vintage Twin Lights labels on limited-edition T-shirts, with the proceeds going to the Thacher Island Association to help maintain the island where the iconic Twin Lighthouses reside—the same lighthouses that adorn the (now very collectible) bottles that must continuously be returned so Pierce is able to keep up production.

As we sip through the history of Rockport, let us appreciate Pierce Sears's dedication to keeping this family-owned business operating and enjoy this wonderful book, which shall serve as a great big "thank-you" to our friend who has quenched the thirst of so many on Cape Ann.

—Philip Elliott Hopkins
Co-executor, The Twin Lights Trust

THE TWIN LIGHTS STORY

I remember my first Twin Lights soda experience after moving to Rockport in 1997. It was at a small seventy-seat movie theater called the Little Arts Cinema just down the street from the bottling plant on the corner of School Street and Broadway in Spiran Hall. The theater is operated by Arnie Morton, who sold the tickets, made the popcorn and sold the refreshments and ran the projector. I remember buying my popcorn one night and asked Arnie if he had any soft drinks. He pointed over his shoulder to a vintage 1950s white refrigerator in the corner and said, "In there, help yourself." Opening the door, I saw an array of small eight-ounce glass bottles with caps that indicated the flavors. I was excited to see that he had many of my favorite flavors not often available in grocery stores, such as birch beer, cream soda and sarsaparilla. These bottles required the use of a bottle opener (no twist-offs for this brand), which Arnie had hung on a long cord on the side of the fridge.

When Pierce Sears asked if I would consider helping to write a book about his company, I knew why he asked. First, as president of the Thacher Island Association, he wanted to pick my brain about the history of Thacher Island's twin lights. Second, he knew I had some soft drink industry and writing experience. A writer by the name of Dev Sherlock and I collaborated on this project. He and I shared interviews with Pierce Sears. We also shared input into the script and researched various elements while Dev researched the Sears and Wilson families. I was tasked with finding most of the photographs, contributing industry details and expanding the text with local historical facts. Working with Pierce and Dev, I harkened back to memories of the soft drink company for which I worked for thirty years, A&W Brands. As vice-president of advertising and promotion, I made annual "roadshow" trips to our franchise bottlers across the nation. My job was to present our new television commercials, marketing strategies and promotional programs in support of our franchise bottler network. My company had purchased and developed several smaller local brands such as Vernor's Ginger Ale and Squirt, along with A&W Root Beer and Cream soda and diet versions of all these brands. I have incorporated some of my experience in these brands into this book to give a fuller view of the soft drink industry and as a comparison to Twin Lights Beverage's place in its history.

In an ironic twist of fate, I was further reminded of my frequent visits to my grandparents' house when I was five years old. My favorite part of the trip was my grandfather giving me bottles of Hires Root Beer. He always kept a stash for me, as neither he nor my grandmother drank it. I am happy to say that during my stint as advertising head with A&W Root Beer, we made it the bestselling root beer in the nation, and I am proud to say it still is today. (Charles Hires formulated and sold the first root beer in this country in 1876.)

The history of the Twin Lights brand is a fascinating look at a success story forged by a determined immigrant family that took a risk, built a business and developed a quality product that has endured for over one hundred years.

Each year, Pierce Sears donates bottles of Twin Lights soda to our Thacher Island Association annual meetings, thus assuring great attendance by the public. Thanks again, Pierce.

—Paul St.Germain
President Emeritus
Thacher Island Association

INTRODUCTION

On a warm spring day in May 1907, the first bottle of Twin Lights carbonated soda water was filled, corked and placed into a rugged wood crate on the floor. The crate was marked "The Consolidated Bottling Works, Rockport, Mass."

Outside, a bright sun was shining down on this small coastal town situated forty miles up the coast from Boston. The previous week had been unseasonably chilly. But the local *Gloucester Times* newspaper had forecast "decidedly summer-like" weather this week, and Mother Nature did not disappoint. Indeed, the thermometer would hit seventy-five degrees that very afternoon.

This felt like a good omen for the two men huddled in the back of the small building near the corner of Broadway and Parker Street. A wood structure with green shingles and two thick slabs of granite serving as front steps, it displayed a sign over the window that read "Thomas Wilson & Co, Grocer." In fact, this was perhaps the perfect day for two grocers-turned-budding-soft drink entrepreneurs to be christening their new business venture.

The first man—lean, mustachioed, wearing a large rubber apron over his shirt and trousers—was forty-six-year-old Thomas Wilson, founder and proprietor. His assistant, tall with a light olive complexion, smooth brown hair and dressed in overalls, was twenty-four-year-old Joe Sears, Wilson's eldest stepson and junior business partner.

From these humble beginnings in the back of their tiny neighborhood grocery store, Thomas Wilson and Joe Sears would grow their new bottling

The oldest wood case from 1919 was one of several designs used over the years. *Author's collection.*

works into a successful and beloved local business that still exists—and remains in the family—more than a century later. Today, Twin Lights is the last remaining independent bottler on the North Shore of Massachusetts, and one of only a handful left in the whole of the northeastern United States.

Since 1860, some 36,000 soft drink bottlers have existed at one time or another in North America. As of 2019, U.S. soft drinks are a $38 billion industry. But today there are fewer than 550 bottlers around the country, and 95 percent of that revenue goes to the 50 top companies in the game.

It's one thing to admire these two hitherto common laborers for being visionary enough to start a bottling business at the turn of the twentieth century, when it was still an evolving and unproven industry. But it's an even greater marvel that such a business has managed to survive—and, indeed, thrive—against all odds for more than eleven decades since.

The history of Twin Lights is a classic American tale. Two children of immigrants devoted to achieving their own definition of the American Dream: Building a business, raising a family and serving as an integral part

Right: Thomas Wilson (1860–1932) first ran a grocery store, then opened his bottling company in 1907 in the back of the store. *Pierce Sears collection*.

Below: Joe Sears Sr. (1857–1895) was a fisherman lost at sea in August 1895 at age thirty-seven, leaving behind a wife and five children. *Pierce Sears collection*.

Joe Sears (1883–1949) (*center*) with his grandson Pierce at age twelve and his wife, Mary, in 1944. He was twenty-four when he partnered with Thomas Wilson in 1907. *Pierce Sears collection.*

of the community that afforded them that opportunity. Thomas Wilson and Joe Sears took a chance on a new idea and, with determination and hard work, made it succeed. The Twin Lights family has watched their industry grow, struggle, grow again and consolidate, all the while resisting any offers or temptation to cash out—content instead to live and maintain their local family business in the place that they've loved and called home ever since their ancestors first stepped off the SS *Barque Azor* at the Port of Boston in the summer of 1859 and settled in the t own of Rockport.

The future of this iconic and stalwart brand, however, does now hang in the balance. Pierce Sears, grandson of Joe Sears and current caretaker of Twin Lights, is now into his eighties and the last surviving heir to the operation. There is nobody in line to which he might bequeath the small bottling plant that sits adjacent to his home, on the same street where it began, grandfathered under current town ordinances. What is more, nobody other than Pierce knows the family recipes or how to operate the antiquated and finicky machinery that resides within the plant's one-hundred-year-old walls.

Over the years, there have been opportunities to sell, cash out, merge or even outsource production. But generation after generation, the makers of Twin Lights decided that their independence, quality of life and small place within the community of Rockport, the town they have always known as home, held greater value. This is their story.

Chapter 1

THE WILSON AND SEARS FAMILIES

Joseph Sears, Mary Silva and Thomas Wilson were three children from Rockport, Massachusetts. Their parents all had immigrated to America in 1859 from the Azores. Joseph (born 1857) made the journey as a baby, while Mary (born 1861) and Thomas (born 1860) would both be born in Rockport not long after their parents' arrival.

Their three individual stories are circuitous yet intertwined. They bear recounting, as each would play a significant role, either directly or indirectly, in the unlikely birth of Twin Lights Tonic.

In the latter half of the 1800s, a wave of immigration saw thousands of Portuguese leave for other parts of the world, with significant numbers heading south for South America (Brazil, Uruguay and Argentina) or west for North America (in particular, Canada and the northeastern United States). The coastal areas above and below Boston, known locally as the North and South Shores, received considerable numbers of Portuguese (as did Cape Cod and Rhode Island), and their heritage in these areas today remains robust. This holds particularly true on Cape Ann, an area at the top of the north shore that marks the northern point of Massachusetts Bay and encompasses the towns of Rockport, Gloucester, Essex and Manchester-by-the-Sea.

The Azores, located 850 miles off the coast of Portugal, almost in the middle of the North Atlantic, is an archipelago of nine islands and the home that these three families left behind for the New World. The attraction for Azoreans, predominantly mariners, fishermen and farmers, to a spot like

Cape Ann would seem natural, given its swathes of fertile land, access to the ocean and a familiar rocky coastline. (Of note, countless census entries from this period, including for these particular families, list "Western Islands" as their place of birth, since that is how sailors and natives commonly referred to Flores and Corvo, the Azores' westernmost islands, in earlier centuries.)

After landing in Boston and settling in Rockport, the families became part of a close-knit community of Azoreans, united not only by a common language and culture but also by their common seafaring trades. (Another prominent migrant group in Rockport during this period was arriving from the Nordic countries—Finns and Swedes as well as the Irish escaping the famine and coming not to work the sea but instead as stonecutters in Rockport's bustling granite quarries.)

The harvesting of granite from quarries dug deep in the earth was big business here on Cape Ann from the 1830s through the early twentieth century. Second only to fishing in economic output, for one hundred years the granite trade played a pivotal role in the local economy, providing jobs for many, turning profits for some and generating tons of cut granite that was used on Cape Ann and shipped to ports all along the Atlantic Seaboard and eventually across the nation.

Granite quarrying started slowly in the area in the late eighteenth century with small operators peppered across rocky terrain. Construction of a fort at Castle Island in Boston Harbor in 1798, followed by a jail in nearby Salem in 1813, jump-started the local granite business. During the 1830s and '40s, the trade grew steadily. By the 1850s, the stone business had been firmly established, and Cape Ann granite was known throughout the region. So extensive and awe-inspiring were operations during the second half of the nineteenth century that some observers feared the business might run out of stone.

While granite was taken from the earth in all different sizes and shapes, Cape Ann specialized in the conversion of that granite into paving blocks, which were used to finish roads and streets. Millions of paving stones were shipped out of Cape Ann annually, destined for construction projects in New York, Philadelphia, New Orleans and San Francisco. The cutting of paving stones kept Gloucester and Rockport workers busy throughout the year but particularly during the winter months. (It was said that granite was more difficult to wrestle out of the earth during winter, hence the cutting of paving blocks out of larger pieces of stone was something that kept men employed during the cold months.) Come summer, large shipments of blocks would be packed aboard specially designed sloops and transported to distant ports.

Paving stones were the major granite quarry product. Millions were created and sent to cities on the East and West Coasts, to New Orleans, Cuba and Paris. *Sandy Bay Historical Society*.

The quarries of Cape Ann were numerous; at least sixty were worked from the mid-1800s until 1930, when the Rockport Granite Company went out of business.

The granite companies consisted of two-man motions as well as large ones employing from 800 to 1,200 workers each over the years. A motion was a small quarry usually operated by two men who cut paving stones to sell themselves or to the big quarry companies. Most workers were immigrants who came from Ireland, Finland, Sweden, Scotland and Italy.

Spiran Hall was mentioned in the foreword. This is a lodge of the Vasa Order of America, a fraternal society originally established for the benefit of Swedish immigrants more than a century ago. It was instituted on April 6, 1906, in Rockport. It is one of a few lodges in the United States that owns its building. Spiran Hall is now dedicated to preserving and sharing Scandinavian and Nordic culture and heritage and is still active today, with many Swedish, Norwegian, Danish, Finnish and Icelandic members and their spouses. It still houses the L'il Arts Theater.

Growing up in the same neighborhood, surrounded by relatives, Mary was a year younger than Thomas and a friend of Thomas's younger sister. (One of their neighbors at the time, just a few doors away, was septuagenarian Hannah Jumper, renowned leader of the local temperance movement's "Hatchet Gang" and a historic Rockport figure.) It was said that Mary and Thomas had begun to take a shine to each other as they approached adolescence. But any chance of a budding romance was abruptly thwarted when Thomas's father uprooted the Wilson family in pursuit of farmwork, leaving Rockport behind for greener pastures in the early 1870s.

Meanwhile, a teenage Joseph Sears had, like his father, taken to the sea, working aboard a fishing schooner. In the intervening years, he and Mary Silva had developed a relationship and in 1880 made things official. On February 1 of that year, Mary and Joseph Sears were married at St. Joachim's Roman Catholic Church in Rockport. She had recently turned eighteen and he, twenty-three.

Thomas Wilson's family, meanwhile, had headed northwest, eighty miles and about a day's journey away, to the town of New Ipswich, New Hampshire. Originally founded by sixty inhabitants from Ipswich, Massachusetts (hence the name), New Ipswich at this time was riding high on America's "Second Industrial Revolution" (a period when many of the newer innovations from earlier in the century finally achieved large-scale adoption and growth, leading to a factory boom). Where factories were built depended on where a means of energy could be accessed. New Ipswich had become a desirable spot thanks to the Souhegan River, a tributary of the Merrimack River, which provided waterpower for several mills, including the state's first woolen mill, a sawmill, a gristmill and a cotton mill.

The Wilsons did not land in New Ipswich inadvertently, and this is where the connections begin to crisscross before taking their eventual shape. A fourth family that had traveled from the Azores along with Joseph Sears's parents, Thomas Wilson's parents and Mary Silva's parents, was a couple named Joseph and Mary Ann Silva. This couple was related to both Thomas Wilson and Mary Silva (now Sears). Joseph Silva was Mary Silva's uncle (her father's brother); his wife, Mary Ann, was Thomas Wilson's aunt (his mother's sister). In fact, the 1865 census shows the Wilsons sharing a dwelling with Joseph and Mary Ann Silva for a short time after their arrival in Rockport. This fourth couple, Joseph and Mary Ann Silva, was the first to decamp to New Hampshire; the Wilsons followed a few years later. This soon becomes relevant.

In 1873, not long after relocating, tragedy struck, as Thomas Wilson's father died. Thomas had just turned thirteen and suddenly found himself living (along with his two siblings and mother) with Aunt Mary Ann and Uncle

Joseph, who had taken them in. But he would make the most of the situation. Joseph had opened a small grocery store and gave Thomas work in the store, first as a stock boy and then as a clerk, slowly teaching him all facets of the business. Thomas spent several years working in the store (as did his sister), learning everything he could along the way. On reaching his twenties, he went to work in the local cotton mill, where he learned to be a machinist, but he still came home to put in time at the store with his uncle, using up whatever tiny bit of energy he had left after a day of laboring in the mill.

Back in Rockport, newlyweds Joseph and Mary (Silva) Sears had settled into a small house together near Pigeon Cove and proceeded to give birth to five children, each a perfect eighteen months apart. Their firstborn was also named

Dory seine net fishing was a lucrative and dangerous occupation, especially on the Grand Banks. *Cape Ann Museum.*

Joseph, after his father and grandfather. (None of these men, frustratingly, ever employed such useful identifiers as "Junior" or "III"; thankfully, for our story, this younger Joseph became known simply as "Joe" Sears.)

Joseph senior continued to ply his trade in the cold Atlantic waters off Cape Ann. It was a bountiful time for fishermen. This was the heyday of the area's fishing industry, boasting more than three hundred schooners manned by some 3,500 men and boys. The immediate area provided plenty of fresh catch, while farther away, the Grand Banks afforded extraordinary stocks of cod and haddock.

Cape Ann was intimately tied to the sea. Incorporated in 1642, the Massachusetts town of Gloucester has been one of the centers of the North Atlantic fishing industry for centuries. In addition to the giant fishing industry, many shipyards dotted the area building hundreds of schooners. Lighthouses also marked the many harbor entrances. There are six major lighthouses on Cape Ann in a six-square-mile area, indicating how dangerous the seas around the Cape are.

Cape Ann has seen more than its fair share of heartbreak. The area grew rapidly in the 1800s, as it provided a convenient launching point for trips to the fertile offshore fishing grounds of George's Bank and the Grand Banks. Gloucester fishermen sailed in specially designed schooners optimized for speed and holding capacity to reach the banks, fill up on cod and other fish and return as quickly as possible. Many of these ship designs were unsafe and prone to capsizing in bad weather. The Fisherman's Memorial *Man at the Wheel* statue on Stacy Boulevard in Gloucester memorializes the 3,880 men lost from 1860 to 1906. Over 1,000 ships were lost, including 265 with all hands. In total, over 5,368 men were lost from the beginning of the fishing industry dating to the 1600s to today.

In the twentieth century, Gloucester fishermen switched from schooners to motorized trawlers. Yet the profession remained hazardous. As recently as April 2020, a crewman of the fishing dragger *Miss Sandy*, Nicolo Vitale, forty-nine, fell from the boat in forty-five-degree water out near Stellwagen Bank about three miles from Gloucester. Although rescued, he died of hypothermia on the way to the hospital in Gloucester.

But tragedy soon struck here in Rockport, too. Joseph Sears would die at sea in August 1895. When his body was returned to shore, the cause of death was determined to be typhoid fever, according to town records dated August 27, 1895. He was only thirty-seven and left behind his wife and five children, ages four to twelve.

In the wake of this tragedy (and, perhaps, a twist of fate), Mary and her children would leave behind their home in Rockport, possessions in hand, and make the daylong journey to New Ipswich, New Hampshire, where her uncle Joseph Silva and his wife, Mary Ann, had agreed to look after them, just as they had done for Thomas Wilson's family. There, Mary was reunited with Thomas; any past romance that may have existed seems to have quickly rekindled. The following year, Thomas Wilson and Mary (Silva) Sears were married on June 7, 1896, in New Ipswich.

Soon, Mary was pregnant with their first son, and the newlywed couple began plotting a return to their beloved Rockport, once Thomas could save up a bit of money working at the mill. By 1900, they were back in Rockport, now a family of eight, crowded into a two-story Colonial with weather-beaten gray wood shingles and a big central fireplace located on the eastern end of Parker Street (just a five-minute walk from where the Twin Lights plant stands today, in fact).

It was a hardscrabble existence at first, with Thomas doing carpentry work, his stepson Joe Sears (now seventeen) working on a nearby farm and stepson John (only fifteen) taking work as a quarryman for the Rockport Granite Company.

But Thomas Wilson had a plan.

Chapter 2
A SHORT HISTORY OF SOFT DRINKS

The origin of the soft drink goes back centuries, to at least the 1300s, when people first ascribed health benefits to consuming, and bathing in, the fizzy mineral waters that bubbled up out of natural springs in the ground. Later, in fifteenth-century England, plain water is known to have been fermented with fruit and flowers (such as elderberry and dandelion) or flavored using citrus, roots and spices. Eventually, in the nineteenth century, these practices would be joined.

In its basic form, the concept of the soft drink has remained relatively unchanged since its inception: bubbly water, sweetened and flavored. What has changed are the method, process and, most profoundly, the business aspects of producing a carbonated soft drink (CSD in today's industry parlance). Filling your cup with soda at a fast-food restaurant, where you can watch the syrup and seltzer eject from a spigot and magically mix together to create a pleasing, refreshing drink, is but a modern automation of the drink's original nineteenth-century process, whereby your local apothecary would manually stir their secret syrup recipe with some bubbly water that had been aerated via a homespun chemical process (more on which later).

There are two distinct aspects to modern soft drink production. On one side is the manufacture of flavoring and syrup. On the other side is bottling and distribution. While recent decades have seen the two sides of the business increasingly consolidated under a same parent company, their two distinct roles remain, effectively, the same today as they were in the beginning.

As of this decade, about 150 companies in the nation produce flavoring syrup and concentrate. These companies then sell that product to soft drink producers (that is, bottlers). Flavoring syrup and concentrate manufacturing are a roughly $8 billion industry, with two familiar names (the Coca-Cola Company and PepsiCo) controlling about 75 percent of the business. And most bottlers today are contractually bound to purchasing proprietary syrup/concentrate from specific producers (like Coca-Cola or Pepsi).

On the bottling and distribution side (remember, Twin Lights was originally called Consolidated Bottling Works, and this is the side of the business on which they've always traded), you have the soft drink producers who actually combine the ingredients (for example, syrup and carbonated water), bottle it and distribute/sell it. As of this decade, there were roughly 500 such outfits in the United States, compared to at least seven times that number (more than 3,500) in the early 1950s, an era commonly acknowledged as the bottling industry's peak. Very few of these remaining bottlers are independent; fewer still are family owned. Twin Lights is one of them.

But how did we get here? Basically, it all started with sparkling water.

For centuries, people traveled to, and coveted, natural springs for the clean, effervescent and mineral-infused waters that they served up from deep within the earth. Naturally, people also spent centuries trying to work out what was in these magical waters, what made them bubbly and, for goodness sake, how they could be re-created.

For our purposes, things really kicked off with the latter stages of these experiments in the late 1700s, when scientists, thinkers and tinkerers around Europe began closing in on ways to artificially re-create fizzy mineral waters. Of course, alcoholic drinks containing carbonation (which occurs naturally via the fermentation process) had already been around for centuries. Beer, for example, dates to at least 3000 BC, according to historians, while champagne dates to the AD 1500s (about the same time it was becoming popular in England for people to flavor their as-yet-uncarbonated water with ingredients such as lemon, cinnamon, rosewater and violets, as mentioned before). But between the growing popularity of resort spas and a growing temperance trend, people wanted healthy, nonalcoholic bubbly water.

Among the key researchers at the time was William Brownrigg, a British doctor who was carrying out health studies on the gases being inhaled by Welsh coal miners. During a visit to a German spa, his interest was piqued by the gases occurring naturally in the mineral water. In 1765, he managed to successfully produce artificially carbonated water using carbon dioxide taken from a nearby mine.

Sparkling water was the first product produced by Wilson Bottling Company. *Author's collection.*

Two years later in Leeds, England, a veritable Renaissance man named Joseph Priestley (chemist, philosopher, teacher, theologian and the person historically credited with discovering oxygen) was experimenting with his own method for infusing water with carbon dioxide. It was based on creating

Joseph Priestley was credited with discovering oxygen as well as inventing a method of infusing water with carbon dioxide to create sparling water. *Wikimedia Commons.*

a chemical reaction to produce gas and then forcing that gas into water. Priestley was quite chuffed with his new discovery and shared the water with friends, noting its "peculiar satisfaction" in his writings. He eventually published a paper titled "Directions for Impregnating Water with Fixed Air" in 1772, for which he won the acclaim of the British Royal Society.

That same year, he provided these instructions to Captain James Cook and his crew for their second voyage to the South Seas, believing it to be a cure for scurvy. It was not. But it would not be the last time that medicinal qualities were falsely attributed to carbonated drinks (more on which later). Nor would it be the start of any great commercial enterprise for Priestley, as he had other things to do (like start a new church).

However, it had certainly captured the imagination of a few other interested parties, one of whom was a Swiss watchmaker-turned-scientist named Johan Jacob Schweppe.

Chemists and scientists around Europe would continue to experiment with, augment and improve on Priestley's discovery, and a few of them even began selling the beverage out of their chemist shops. Schweppe, for example, developed a variation on Priestley's carbonation method that he called the "Geneva Process." He established the Schweppes Company in 1783 in Switzerland before later moving it to London (where he was eventually appointed official supplier to the royal family). The rest is pretty much history.

By 1791, Priestley's controversial political and religious beliefs saw him effectively chased out of England (an angry mob burning down his house was apparently the final straw), and he ended up living out the rest of his life near Philadelphia, which also just happened to be one of the early hubs (along with New York and Boston) of the burgeoning mineral water trade in America. It is believed to have started, however, in New Haven, Connecticut. A chemistry professor at Yale, Benjamin Silliman, was a faithful convert to the perceived healing properties of natural spring water, having spent time at the Saratoga and Ballston Springs in

Johan Schweppe developed a variation of Priestley's method called the "Geneva Process." He started the Schweppes Company in 1783 in Switzerland.
Schweppes website.

Upstate New York. By 1800 in England, the artificial mineral water trade had advanced enough that one could now purchase an apparatus that would create artificially carbonated water, so Silliman ordered one and had it shipped over. In 1806, after some time experimenting with his new machine, Silliman opened what is believed to be the earliest "soda fountain" in the United States (which he later relocated to New York City before eventually going out of business and losing money for the investors who had backed his big push into the big city.)

But artificial bubbly water was now gaining momentum in America. The first patent for "imitation mineral water" was issued in the United States in 1809. A decade later, in 1819, a patent for the "soda fountain" was granted. Still, the novelty of the product at this point was simply the ability to enjoy bubbly water (and, perhaps, its healing properties) at a shop in the middle of town, without traveling to a natural spring out in the country. At first, these "fountains" focused on re-creating the actual chemical makeup of mineral waters from certain famous springs, such as the Seltzer Spring in Germany (famously high in calcium, chloride, magnesium, sulfate and potassium ions, and the spring that begat the generic term "seltzer") or the Saratoga Spring in New York (high in bicarbonate, calcium, magnesium and iron). The latter had a milder flavor profile than its European counterparts, and it was famously favored by the likes of Nathaniel Hawthorne and Edgar Allen Poe.

Back in Philadelphia, however, a Frenchman named Eugene Roussel was about to change that. A perfumer by trade, Roussel had set up a soda fountain in his shop and, in 1839, began selling lemon-flavored soda water. (Roussel is also believed to be one of the first to bottle a flavored water a few years later.) The addition of lemon flavoring, which Roussel had essentially borrowed from lemonade street vendors in his native Paris, proved so popular that it quickly inspired (or, perhaps, forced) other soda fountain operators to start keeping their own flavored extracts on hand, such as lemon, ginger and teaberry.

Soon, vendors everywhere were adding flavors (later, even ice cream) to their carbonated water. Soda-dispensing fountain machines continued to

Today's coffee baristas play a similar role as a soda jerk did back then. *Library of Congress.*

appear in hotels, candy shops, apothecaries and cafés—in many ways, the same places where coffee vendors now dominate today. American fountain manufacturers touted their apparatus as "one of the most beneficial additions to an existing business...ornamental and at the same time profitable."

The experience of being served a soda drink then, from an elaborate machine by a skilled attendant, furthers the comparison to coffee vending today, where one might have a coffee shop barista prepare a fresh-pressed cappuccino with steamed milk. In both cases, the experience was almost as much about the performance and preparation of the drink as it was about the drink itself.

Outside of the big cities, as the century progressed, a similar setup, in the form of "soda counters," was soon becoming a standard feature at local pharmacies and corner drugstores around the rest of the country. No longer a novelty reserved for cosmopolitan city dwellers, these new small-town soda counters became a popular meeting place where residents would gather and socialize while the aroma from the fruits, spices and other flavoring ingredients perfumed the air. Poole's pharmacy on Main Street in Rockport, with its striped awning and "SODA" in large letters on the side, served as one such place for much of the twentieth century.

This led to an industry-transforming development for soft drinks. Now the pharmacists were really getting involved with the process, mixing up both flavors and remedies. The practice would give birth to some of the most prominent brands in the history of soft drinks.

An old-fashioned soda fountain in at Collins Pharmacy, Islip, New York, in 1915. *Library of Congress*.

Poole's Drug Store with its green-striped awning and the large letters "Soda" on it on Main Street, Rockport. *Sandy Bay Historical Society*.

When I made marketing presentations to our A&W franchised bottlers, I often told the story of how A&W got started in 1919 in Lodi, California. A man by the name of Roy W. Allen had partnered with his friend Frank Wright to sell their own brand of draft root beer in a parking lot at a parade for returning World War I veterans. They sold hot dogs as well and encouraged the crowd to "drive-thru" the lot to pick up their food and soft drinks without leaving their cars. Frank had recently purchased the formula for a root beer flavor from a pharmacist in Arizona.

By 1923, they had opened their first drive-in restaurant in Sacramento, California. The company name was taken from the initials of their last names: Allen and Wright. The A&W brand became famous for its "Frosty Mugs," in which the mugs would be kept in the freezer and filled with A&W Root Beer. Eventually, the franchise developed into the first successful fast food–franchising operation. A&W had its root beer concentrate made by a wholly owned subsidiary, J. Hungerford Smith, which today is owned by Conagra. J. Hungerford Smith himself began his flavors and toppings business in 1879 as a pharmacist in his own drugstore.

In 1971, A&W Beverages Inc. was formed as a subsidiary of United Brands (formerly United Fruit Company), which had bought the A&W restaurants and trademark and began supplying bottled A&W products to grocery stores via a national network of over two hundred franchised soft

A&W got started in 1919 in Lodi, California, eventually becoming the first drive-in restaurant featuring root beer floats. *Author's collection.*

A&W's first drive-in was established in Sacramento, California, in 1923, eventually growing to over two thousand locations by the 1960s. *Author's collection.*

drink bottlers. In 1985, A&W Cream soda was introduced as well as diet versions of both flavors.

A&W was one of hundreds of soft drink brands caught up in the consolidation of the industry in the late 1990s, as alluded to in chapter 11.

A&W Beverages was eventually folded into Cadbury Beverages in 1993, which would spin it off to Dr. Pepper/ 7UP in 2008 and is now under the Keurig Dr Pepper umbrella of brands.

A&W FOUNTAIN BUSINESS

In the 1920s, A&W restaurants jumped on the soda fountain bandwagon by offering fresh-made root beer made each day in each of their restaurants. The restaurants also encouraged take-home packages of root beer in specially made wax-coated paper bottles in the form of a megaphone. These packages held a full quart. Over time, the company added one-gallon take-home glass bottles, which could be returned and refilled (before strict FDA rules were imposed). What made the restaurant product so good was that they used pure cane sugar, no preservatives, and a lower carbonation level than the later canned and bottled product sold in retail stores. To this day, the unique blend of herbs, spices, barks and berries remains a proprietary secret.

The formulation included varying amounts of vanilla, sarsaparilla root, licorice, birch bark, wintergreen and anise. All of this served to provide the drinker with a smooth-tasting root beer that became synonymous with the frozen glass mugs the restaurants served it in, providing what eventually became the brand's singular advertising slogan, "Get that Frosty Mug Taste."

A&W was one of the first franchised restaurant chains in the United States. It is amazing to realize that an entire fast-food chain was developed based on a single root beer flavored soda and a new byproduct called the A&W Root Beer Float. Over the years, A&W restaurants were bought and sold many times. At one time in the 1960s, over two thousand restaurants existed in the United States, Canada and Asia.

Vernor's Ginger Ale is another example of a pharmacist-created business. Vernor's Ginger Ale was bought by United Brands in 1979 and eventually sold in 1987 to A&W Brands to add to its portfolio of strong regional brands such as Squirt (a grapefruit-flavored soft drink). Vernor's was the bestselling ginger ale in Michigan and especially the Detroit area. It goes back before

A&W restaurants sold root beer in paper cartons in the form of a megaphone. *Author's collection.*

Coke, Pepsi, Hires or Moxie. James Vernor was a pharmacist in Detroit in 1866, opening his drugstore after serving in the Civil War. Over 140 years old, Vernor's Ginger Ale is America's oldest continuously produced soft drink.

Its growth followed a similar route to popularity that Thomas Wilson's Twin Light soda did. The only difference was that Vernor had developed his formulation almost by mistake. He had experimented with his formulation before he left for the war. On his return, he opened a wood cask of his extract and found that he had the taste he had been hoping for. The secret formula and the four years aging in wood casks had perfected his ginger ale and gave it a "Deliciously Different" flavor.

By 1896, he had established a small plant down the street from his now closed drugstore. The plant was devoted to blending, aging and bottling Vernor's. Also that year, a horse and a wagon were purchased for distribution purposes, and in the beginning, the father and son were the only employees.

The demand for Vernor's was huge. Every first-class drugstore in Detroit installed dispensing equipment specifically to serve Vernor's. Hospitals began utilizing it, and thousands of cases were delivered to homes. This sounds similar to how Twin Lights was received here in Rockport. Eventually, Vernor's began to offer its extract to franchise bottlers in the area. Regrettably, Thomas Wilson decided to not franchise his brand but produce and distribute it himself.

Moxie, for example, was originally created as a patent medicine called "Moxie Nerve Food" by Dr. Augustin Thompson from Union, Maine, in 1876. It was initially produced in Lowell, Massachusetts. Moxie's flavor is unique, a sweet drink with a bitter aftertaste. It is flavored with gentian root extract, an extremely bitter substance commonly used in herbal medicine. Thompson originally claimed that it helped fight paralysis, softening of the brain, nervousness and insomnia. Thompson claimed he named it after a Lieutenant Moxie, a purported friend of his who, Thompson claimed, had discovered the plant. Other stories claimed that the name likely derives

Left: Vernor's Ginger Ale was created by James Vernor, a pharmacist. He developed an extract that was aged in wood casks to perfect the flavor. *Author's collection*.

Below: Vernor bought his first delivery wagon, and he and his son delivered extract to drugstores and soda fountains around Detroit in 1896. *Author's collection*.

Moxie was created as a patent medicine called "Moxie Nerve Food" by a doctor in Maine in 1876. *Library of Congress.*

from an Abenaki word that means "dark water" and is found in lake and river names in Maine. By 1884, he had begun selling it in bottles and in bulk as a soda fountain syrup. This is when he added soda water to the flavor syrup, and it became a unique-tasting soft drink. Most people find the flavor hard to describe—from root beer and cola to sarsaparilla and Vernor's Ginger Ale, to black licorice, birch beer and cough syrup.

Although Moxie reached most of the country at its peak—Frank Potter, who wrote several books of Moxie history, has lived all his ninety years in Paducah, Kentucky—its roots remain in New England. Potter relates a story that may or may not be true. When Warren Harding died in 1923, his vice president, Calvin Coolidge, was at the family farm in Vermont bailing hay. The telegraph messenger arrived at 2:00 a.m. with the news, and old John Coolidge, a justice of the peace, swore in his son as president of the United States. They toasted the event with Moxie. True or not, it is an interesting story.

Moxie is now owned by Coca-Cola.

Dr Pepper was created at a corner drugstore in Waco, Texas, in 1885, where Charles Alderton (not actually a doctor, but a pharmacist) combined

THE extreme care—the hygienic cleanliness—used in making as well as shipping Dr. Pepper, means a lot to you.

Drink

Dr. Pepper

— TRADE MARK —

KING OF BEVERAGES

Free From Caffeine

A Universal Coupon Given with Each Glass

Healthful   Thirst-Quenching   Satisfying

DR. PEPPER COMPANY, WACO, TEXAS

Dr Pepper advertised in a beverage trade journal to sell its flavor extract to bottlers as a caffeine-free, healthful and thirst-quenching product. *American Bottler Magazine.*

some twenty-three different ingredients in an effort to create a new flavor for the store's soda counter, because, the story goes, customers had grown bored of the standard sarsaparilla, vanilla and lemon options.

A year after that, in 1886, Coca-Cola was introduced by a pharmacist at the Eagle Drug and Chemical House in Columbus, Georgia (where it was originally promoted as "Ideal Brain Tonic and Sovereign Remedy for Headache and Nervousness") by Dr. John Pemberton. He later sold the formula to Asa Candler (yes, another pharmacist) in 1887. The Coca-Cola brand was appropriate, as the secret formula did include a small amount of cocaine. Coca-Cola was named in 1885 for its two "medicinal" ingredients: extract of coca leaves and kola nuts. Just how much cocaine was originally in the formulation is hard to determine, but the drink undeniably contained some cocaine in its early days. Frederick Allen describes the public attitude toward cocaine that existed as Coca-Cola's developers worked on perfecting their formula in 1891:

> *The first stirrings of a national debate had begun over the negative aspects of cocaine, and manufacturers were growing defensive over charges that use of their products might lead to "cocainism" or the "cocaine habit." The full-throated fury against cocaine was still a few years off, and Candler was anxious to continue promoting the supposed benefits of the coca leaf, but there was no reason to risk putting more than a tiny bit of coca extract in their syrup. He cut the amount to a mere trace.*

But neither could Asa Candler take the simple step of eliminating the fluid extract of coca leaves from the formula. Candler believed that his product's name had to be descriptive and that he must have at least some byproduct of the coca leaf in the syrup (along with some kola) to protect his right to the Coca-Cola name. Protecting the name was critical. Candler had no patent on the syrup itself. Anyone could make an imitation. But no one could put the label "Coca-Cola" on an imitation so long as Candler owned the name. The name was the thing of real value,

This 1900s ad for Coca-Cola explains that it is healthful, good for mental and physical exhaustion and for weary and despondent women. *Author's collection.*

and the registered trademark was its only safeguard. Coca leaves had to stay in the syrup.

How much cocaine was in that "mere trace" is impossible to say, but we do know that by 1902 there was as little as 1/400 of a grain of cocaine per ounce of syrup. Coca-Cola did not become completely cocaine-free until 1929, but there was scarcely any of the drug left in the drink by then:

So, yes, at one time there was cocaine in Coca-Cola. But before you're tempted to run off claiming Coca-Cola turned generations of drinkers into dope addicts, consider the following: in 1885, it was far from uncommon to use cocaine in patent medicines (which is what Coca-Cola was originally marketed as) and other medical potions. When it first became general knowledge that cocaine could be harmful, the backroom chemists who comprised the Coca-Cola company at the time (long before it became the huge company we now know) did everything they could with the technology they had at the time to remove every trace of cocaine from the beverage. What was left behind (until the technology improved enough for it all to be removed) was not enough to give a fly a buzz.

7UP was created by Charles Leiper Grigg, who launched his St. Louis–based company, the Howdy Corporation, in 1920. Grigg came up with the formula for a lemon-lime soft drink in 1929. He too became embroiled in the debate as to the safety of one of its ingredients, lithium. The product, originally named "Bib-Label Lithiated Lemon-Lime Soda," was launched two weeks before the Wall Street Crash of 1929. It contained lithium citrate, a mood-stabilizing drug that provided a lift to the drinker. It was one of several patent medicine products popular in the late nineteenth and early twentieth centuries. Its name was later shortened to "7 Up Lithiated Lemon Soda" before being further shortened to "7UP" in 1938. By 1948, lithium had been removed from the formula.

The origin of the 7UP name is unclear, but there are several theories. Some claim that it is derived from the seven ingredients used in the original recipe; others, that it is derived from the soda having a pH of 7 (which is not true). Still others think that the "7" originates from the lithium in the original formula, as this element has an atomic mass of ~7. The "UP" refers to the uplifting qualities derived from the lithium. Some believe that it comes from the fact that 7UP was bottled in seven-ounce bottles, as most other soft drinks were bottled in six-ounce bottles. Grigg never revealed how he came up with the name. 7UP is now part of the Keurig family of brands. (See chapter 11 on industry consolidation.)

Pepsi-Cola, too, originated at a pharmacy, this one in New Bern, North Carolina, in 1893. Pepsi was first introduced as "Brad's Drink" by Caleb Bradham, who made it at his drugstore, where the drink was sold. It was renamed Pepsi-Cola in 1898 after the Greek word for "digestion" (πέψις, pronounced "pepsis"), which the drink was purported to aid, and "cola" after the kola nut. The original recipe also included sugar and vanilla. Bradham sought to create a fountain drink that was appealing and would aid in digestion and boost energy.

In 1903, Bradham moved the bottling of Pepsi-Cola from his drugstore to a rented warehouse. That year, he sold 7,968 gallons of syrup. The next year, Pepsi was sold in six-ounce bottles, and sales increased to 19,848 gallons. In 1909, automobile race pioneer Barney Oldfield was the first celebrity to endorse Pepsi-Cola, describing it as "a bully drink…refreshing, invigorating, a fine bracer before a race." The advertising theme "Delicious and Healthful" was then used over the next two decades.

During the Great Depression, Pepsi-Cola gained popularity following the introduction in 1934 of a 12-ounce bottle. Prior to that, Pepsi and Coca-Cola sold their drinks in 6.5-ounce servings for about five cents a bottle. With a radio advertising campaign featuring the popular jingle "Nickel, Nickel"—first recorded by the Tune Twisters in 1940—Pepsi encouraged price-conscious consumers to double the volume their nickels could purchase. The jingle is arranged in a way that loops, creating a never-ending tune: "Pepsi-Cola hits the spot / Twelve full ounces, that's a lot / Twice as much for a nickel, too / Pepsi-Cola is the drink for you." Coming at a time of economic crisis, the campaign succeeded in boosting Pepsi's status. From 1936 to 1938, Pepsi-Cola's profits doubled.

From the 1930s through the late 1950s, "Pepsi-Cola Hits the Spot" was the most commonly used slogan in the days of old radio, classic motion pictures and, later, television. Its jingle (conceived in the days when Pepsi cost only five cents) was used in many different forms with different lyrics. With the rise of radio, Pepsi utilized the services of a young, up-and-coming actress named Polly Bergen to promote products, oftentimes lending her singing talents to the classic "…hits the spot" jingle.

By 2008, according to *Beverage Digest*'s report on soft drinks, PepsiCo's market share was 30.8 percent, while Coca-Cola's was 42.7 percent. Coke outsells Pepsi in most parts of the United States.

A final word on fountains: It bears noting that Boston became a dominant force in the fountain trade, having been home to two of the largest fountain makers in the industry: J.W. Tufts of Charlestown, inventor of the Arctic Soda Fountain; and A.D. Puffer & Sons of Boston. The two companies would create a veritable monopoly of the fountain industry when, in 1891, they merged with John Matthews Company (founded by an Englishman in New York) and Charles Lippincott of Philadelphia to establish the American Soda Fountain Company. The company was run by Tufts in Boston and made everyone involved extremely wealthy.

As for the mixing and consumption of these carbonated treats, it was still being done largely at the point of sale, with the idea of enjoying a

Opposite: Early Pepsi ad promoting its sales strategy of offering twelve ounces instead of six for the same nickel price as other soft drinks. *Author's collection*.

Above: Pepsi has changed its logo many times. The "double dot" between Pepsi and Cola on the right was before 1903, and the more modern one is on the left, in the 1930s. *Author's collection*.

carbonated beverage "off-premises" still more a wishful concept than a practical one. The problem was that it was hard to contain the bubbly waters. For one thing, early glass bottles were prone to breakage under the pressure of the carbonation. An even bigger issue was keeping the gas from escaping. Consumers would attempt to bottle sparkling mineral water at the springs—for example, by sealing it in a ceramic jug with a wet cork and a wax seal—but, inevitably, by the time they'd transported it home, the fizz was mostly gone.

This does not mean people were not still trying to do it and making incremental improvements along the way. As of 1849, there were at least 64 known "bottling works" in the country, according to the U.S. census. By 1859, this number had increased to 123 (with the largest number being in New York City and Philadelphia). The concept at this point had picked up enough steam that American companies, having so far left the manufacture of bottling equipment to the Europeans (who were exporting these wares to America), now finally decided there was enough of a growing "bottler" market to start building bottling machinery here in the United States.

We are still talking about a very rudimentary, hand-and-foot-operated "filling and corking device." But it was progress. By 1869, we were up to 387 plants on record; yet another decade along, in 1879, the U.S. Census Bureau recorded some 512 "Mineral and Soda Water" factories (according to the ever-shifting terminology). The fuse, it appeared, was lit. The trend was now real. And waiting just around the corner were the key innovations that would really set things off.

Chapter 3

SETTING UP SHOP

Boom. By the turn of the twentieth century, the bottling trade was exploding. There were at least one hundred different soft drink brands and more than 2,500 bottling plants around the country. The latter is an eye-opening number, for sure, but it is important to remember that the vast majority of these "plants" were not what we imagine a bottling plant today. These were small mom-and-pop operations, often set up in a garage, a basement or the back of a grocery store. Many were operated only part-time (in warmer months), and most serviced only their (very) immediate geographic area.

Reaffirming the trend, an article in *Goldman's Gazette* in 1905 declared that the bottling trade now had "few equals in other lines of commerce." The publication attributed this to several factors—in particular, growing public demand for the product and complete mechanization of the process, which was making it both easier and more affordable for almost anyone to get into the bottling business. The article continued, "Every requisite, from racking-off to labeling and crating for shipment, has been changed from hand work to rapid mechanical execution that sets aside completely the old objection urged against bottling on the score of expense."

Thomas Wilson was about to become the first-ever bottler to set up shop in Rockport, Massachusetts. But two notable predecessors on Cape Ann, both in the neighboring town of Gloucester, merit mention.

George A. Davis was an inquisitive young man from Gloucester who had been experimenting with fermentation and carbonation. During a spell working in Newburyport, Massachusetts, he met local businessman S.H. Winn, who offered to finance Davis's bottling business. In 1869, Davis, still in his early twenties, returned to Gloucester and established the Winn & Davis Bottling Works (later becoming George A. Davis Bottling Works). Based out of the back of a building on Western Avenue, one block up from the waterfront, he was soon advertising "Mineral Water and Sarsaparilla Beer" as well as "Porters, Ales and Ciders." It was not uncommon during this time for bottlers to produce both soft and hard drinks. But it is notable that he would advertise the alcoholic drinks in rather smaller lettering than his soft drinks, perhaps conscious of the prevailing temperance trend at the time.

Several years later, three sons of a Gloucester fisherman also caught the bottling bug. As teenagers, Gilman and Fitzwilliam Blatchford had followed their older brother Walter to Providence, Rhode Island, where the three worked in a factory making screws. Walter was a machinist and the younger brothers his earnest apprentices. By 1890, the trio had saved a small pool of money and returned home to Gloucester to pursue a new family bottling enterprise. Blatchford Brothers was founded at 140 Washington Street in Gloucester, giving Cape Ann yet another bottling works before the turn of the century. (Note: decades later, the Blatchford Brothers' company will resurface in the Twin Lights story.) For the record, Gloucester town directories during this period list a few other bottlers—Charles M. Kendall, Lane & McClean, C.H. Campbell, Sullivan Bros.—that came and went. It seems the bottling trade was not for everyone.

Meanwhile, however, Thomas Wilson was back in Rockport with his large new family and moving forward with his plan. John Silva, older brother of Mary (Silva Sears) Wilson, had been running a small family grocer in the building that is now 67 Broadway (near Parker Street, one door down from where the Twin Lights plant stands today), but he was ready to give it up and return to fishing. In 1901, Thomas Wilson took over his brother-in-law's store and hung a new sign over the door: "T. Wilson, Groceries." Applying the knowledge, he had accumulated in his uncle's store in New Hampshire all those years, Wilson now had his own business and one employee, Joe Sears, working as a clerk, meat cutter and delivery boy. The original building still stands and is now the home of a creative fabric designer, Parker Brown.

The business did well—so well, in fact, that in 1904, when Dr. Charles F.A. Hall, owner of the large house next door to the store, put his property up for sale, the Wilsons bought it and moved in. (In fact, it was Mary Wilson's name on the deed, which is rather remarkable for the time, as women

Thomas Wilson took over his brother-in-law's store in 1901, renaming it T. Wilson Groceries. Joe Sears worked as his partner, meat cutter and delivery boy. *Pierce Sears collection*.

The building stands today in relatively the same configuration. It is now owned by Parker Brown, a creative fabric designer shop. *Author's collection*.

This is Pierce Sears's home at 71 Broadway. He moved here in 1960 and lives there today. *Author's collection.*

generally were not leading such major transactions. But Mary Wilson was an exceptional woman). That same year, young Joe Sears also got married. On October 30, 1904, he and Mary Bernard, the daughter of a French Canadian blacksmith for the Rockport Granite Company, wed at the same Rockport church where his parents had wed twenty-four years earlier.

Mary Bernard's father would have been an important employee of the granite companies working as a blacksmith. Blacksmiths sharpened stone-cutting equipment, made the equipment, tempered the tools, created new ones and kept the giant derricks in operation and the steel rigging wire intact that supported the derricks. They were so essential to the quarry business that the Cape Tool Company was formed in 1891 to provide blacksmithing operations on a larger scale for all the companies. It was reported that at least one blacksmith was required for each ten to fifteen quarrymen to keep their equipment in top condition. They also made horseshoes for the many horses and mules used by the granite quarry companies.

The year 1906 was also eventful. Joe Sears and his wife gave birth to their first child (and subsequent heir to the Twin Lights business), George

Lewis Sears. Only a few weeks earlier, Thomas and Mary Wilson (Joe's stepfather and mother) had given birth to a daughter, Mary Elizabeth. But 1906 is most notable for being the year that gave birth to the idea of starting a bottling operation. It was a natural accompaniment to any grocery business, after all. Just a year before, for example, a young man named Claud Hatcher had set up a small bottling machine in the basement of his family's grocery store in Columbus, Georgia, the Hatcher Grocery Company. He called it the Union Bottling Works, and his first product, RC Ginger Ale, ended up ultimately launching the RC Cola empire. Although successful with Royal Crown Ginger Ale, he decided that the greatest profits to be made were in the cola marketed by the giant Coca-Cola. He introduced his own cherry-flavored cola called Chero-Cola; by 1911, it was the company's bestselling product. In 1914, Hatcher filed for a trademark for Chero-Cola. Coca-Cola quickly responded, demanding the word *cola* be removed from all advertising. This clash lasted thirty years before it was finally settled after World War II.

After Coke won the case, Hatcher introduced a new brand of soft drink in 1924 that became the Nehi line of fruit-flavored drinks. In 1934, a new brand was introduced named Royal Crown, which was a cola but was not mentioned in the advertising. It was also known as "RC." Finally, in 1944,

Cape Ann Tool Company's resident blacksmiths stand for a photo. One blacksmith could work for ten to fifteen quarrymen, keeping their tools in good condition. *Sandy Bay Historical Society.*

Left: Nehi was introduced in 1924 as a line of fruit flavors; RC was introduced in 1934 (without the word *cola*). *Author's collection.*

Below: An ad for Empire Wagon Works. Note the specific description for each wagon, Plain Body Seltzer or Bottled Beer and Soda Wagon. *American Bottler Magazine.*

Nehi Inc. ultimately prevailed over Coke after a thirty-year legal battle. The courts allowed that the company could use the word *cola*. RC Cola sales took off, and the brand was declared the "Leading New Product of the 1960s." Over the years, RC had been purchased by several investors. It finally became a subsidiary of RC/Arby's Corporation. This was the second time a soft drink was owned by a national restaurant chain. Today, RC Cola is the third-largest cola brand, behind Coke and Pepsi.

Looking around Rockport, there were at least twenty other grocers in 1906, but not one of them had jumped on the bottling boom yet.

Soon, copies of the *American Bottler*, a monthly periodical that served the bottling trade, were arriving in the mail, and Thomas and Joe were studying it intently. In its pages one could find more than one hundred advertisers offering products and services to the independent bottler, everything from extracts and sweeteners to bottle-washing contraptions to wood crates and cork stoppers. Consultants placed classified ads offering their services to aspiring bottlers, while companies like Empire Wagon Works pitched their customized delivery coaches. More than just a buyer's guide, the periodical also delivered news of the latest updates and innovations, as well as practical columns offering legal, marketing and bookkeeping tips for new bottlers going into business for themselves.

American Seltzer clear glass-embossed bottle saved as a memento by Thomas Wilson when he trained there in 1907. *Pierce Sears collection.*

All this research was well and good. But there was still one small catch: They had to figure out how to work this stuff. Thomas Wilson was a practical man. He had learned the grocery trade from the floor up by doing it. He had learned to be a machinist by working in the mill. Now, he would learn the bottling business the same way. And so, the decision was made: Joe Sears would take over the running of the store (and looking after the family), while Thomas went off to learn the bottling trade.

For this, he traveled south to Beverly, Massachusetts, a town eighteen miles down the coast from Rockport. Beverly was home to the America Seltzer Company, which had been founded in the summer of 1897 on

Elliot Street by Meyer Seligman. (American Seltzer Company would later produce tonic under the name Garden City Beverages and managed to stay in business, under a man named Eddie Cantor, until 1972.) Wilson spent four months working in Seligman's plant, learning the machinery, the operation and the business, before returning to Rockport in the spring, just in time for the start of beverage season.

Chapter 4

ROCKPORT, A SUMMER DESTINATION

U ntil the mid-nineteenth century, Rockport was still part of Gloucester. It was a parish of Gloucester called Sandy Bay, as Gloucester was originally established as a series of church parishes in its early years. The residents incorporated it in February 1840, establishing Rockport as a town of its own. In 1839, a vote was taken on the name of the new town. Names considered were Rockport, Cape Ann, East Gloucester and Granite. Rockport won with forty votes; Granite was second with only ten votes.

In addition to its fishing and granite industries, Rockport was by this time developing a third significant industry that continues to thrive to this day: summer tourism.

Key to this development was Eastern Railroad extending its lines into Gloucester and Rockport, enabling direct and easy passage from Boston, New York and beyond. The line was first extended to Gloucester (which enjoyed a sizable tourist trade itself) in 1847, followed by Rockport in 1861 after much rallying by residents. The transport of both visitors and goods via locomotive would prove transformative for the previously somewhat remote peninsula.

As of 1905, shortly before the birth of Twin Lights, the Boston & Maine Railroad was offering sixteen trains daily in the summertime between Boston's North Station and Gloucester (with express trains making the trip in less than an hour). Visitors could also now get to Cape Ann by automobile ("over a fine stretch of State Highway and Ocean Boulevard," read a Cape Ann Chamber of Commerce pamphlet) or by boat, via the Boston and

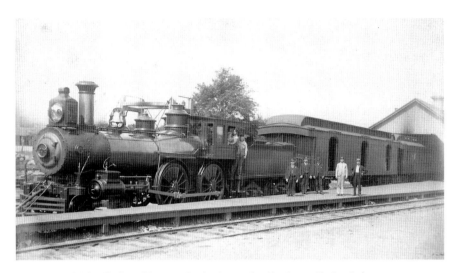

A Boston & Maine Railroad locomotive in the yard at Rockport. It shuttled passengers to and from Boston daily in 1905. *Sandy Bay Historical Society*.

The ferry SS *Cape Ann* ran from Gloucester to Boston daily for only fifty cents each way. *Sandy Bay Historical Society*.

Gloucester Steamboat Company. From June to September, the SS *Cape Ann* ("The Pride of the North Shore") would ferry passengers between Boston and Gloucester, a two-hour sail, for the price of fifty cents each way.

So, by the time Thomas Wilson bottled his first mineral water in 1907, Rockport was dotted with hotels, guest houses and private summer homes. Arrivals at the train depot were met by a queue of horse-drawn carriages

Ocean View House in Pigeon Cove was one of the most sought-after vacation sites with its seventy-five rooms. *Sandy Bay Historical Society.*

waiting to transport guests, for a sum of twenty-five cents, to destinations in Pigeon Cove such as the Glen Acre on Granite Street and the Ocean View House with its seventy-five rooms and elegant parlors (located, per its 1903 brochure, "at the extreme northeast point of Cape Ann...where the sea is wild, and the winds are free"). Perhaps visitors would be destined for the more famous Turk's Head Inn at Land's End on South Street. The area's most grand hotel at the time, it would, over the years, play host to admirals, celebrities and dignitaries—each with a summer thirst to quench.

Besides tourists and vacationers, the town played host to the U.S. Navy each summer.

The years between 1889 and 1920 saw the frequent arrival of the navy's North Atlantic Fleet each summer for fleet exercises. In 1906, a fleet led by Rear Admiral Robley "Fighting Bob" Evans aboard his flagship USS *Maine* arrived. He brought two divisions of the North Atlantic Fleet, which included the battleships USS *Alabama*, *Kearsarge*, *Iowa*, *Missouri*, *Illinois*, *Indiana* and *Kentucky* and the gun boat *Yankton*. Admiral Evans was a high-profile naval officer, having once individually commanded all of the battleships just mentioned as well as the *Connecticut* and *Ohio* and the cruiser *New York* between 1895 and 1907. He also commanded a squadron of the Great White Fleet that sailed around the world from 1907 to 1909.

In the summer of 1906, over thirty-five warships filled the harbor at Sandy Bay overlooking Thacher Island. Each battleship carried a complement of four hundred to six hundred officers and crew.

This visit brought the most battleships ever to Sandy Bay. Evans arrived in June and did not leave until August. He and his crews were entertained and given the run of the town, and special arrangements were made for crew members at the town hall. The crews accounted for over five thousand men, equal to the population of Rockport at the time. The postmaster, "Uncle" Bill Parson, was quoted as saying, "on each mail the letters and packages came in voluminous quantities. This morning's mail brought over 5000 pieces." Several family members of the crews were put up at local hotels, including the Turk's Head Inn, Ocean View House, Edward Hotel, Hawthorne Inn Casino, and many stayed at private homes made available by the locals for extra cash. Banquets, dinners and receptions were held all over town. Baseball games at the South End, Winter's Field and Webster's Field were numerous, featuring town teams as well as teams from the ships. In return, the ships put on spectacular searchlight exhibitions and each ship's band played on board as well as at various hotels. Fully ten thousand people came for the searchlight displays. The ships set up visitations and ferry service from T-Wharf on many afternoons so that hundreds of citizens could board the ships. This was a significant sampling opportunity for Twin Lights Tonic.

Sailors were welcomed by the townspeople, who turned the town hall into a dormitory and meeting place for the crew members. Fifty cots were

The U.S. Navy's North Atlantic Fleet anchored in Sandy Bay. From left to right: battleships *Missouri, Kearsarge, Alabama, Maine* and *Illinois. Sandy Bay Historical Society.*

The electric trolly leaving Rockport with sailors to play baseball with local teams at Webster Field. *Sandy Bay Historical Society.*

set up in the auditorium, and writing desks, souvenir letterheads and pens, ice cream, coffee, soft drinks, donuts and reading matter were provided. The lawns were decked out with electric lights so the men could gather at night. Wilson provided the soft drinks for the troops.

Sailors crowd onto the electric trolley car on their way to Gloucester for shore leave and baseball. In the accompanying image, note the baseball players in their uniforms. More than 1,550 sailors took liberty that day, many drinking Twin Lights Tonic at the ballpark.

Thousands came to visit the ships each day. Ships were usually open from 1:00 p.m. until 5:00 p.m., and the ships' launches picked up visitors at T-Wharf to ferry them to the ships. Many private boats got into the action as well and did very well for themselves financially for the two months the fleet was in town. Thomas Wilson also did well, selling his cold tonic on the docks.

Tourism continues to be a large part of the economic scene in Rockport. The average winter population is about 7,500 residents and expands to around 20,000 during the summer months.

Chapter 5

ROCKPORT'S FIRST BOTTLER

On May 22, 1907, two weeks after Thomas Wilson and Joe Sears bottled their first cases of soda water, a small notice appeared in the *Gloucester Times*, under the Rockport news section of the paper in the "Local and Personal" column: "The Consolidated Bottling Works, a new industry, has its delivery teams out establishing routes. Mr. Thomas Wilson is the manager and the works are on his premises on Broadway."

Establishing retail outlets was important. Unless there was a special community event or church gathering, the only places people could get the product in those days was at their small neighborhood grocer, which were numerous. (It was the opposite for bottlers out West, who typically had only a single, albeit large, general store.) People did not have access to big supermarkets or box stores like they do today. Nearly everything they needed was purchased in the neighborhood, and Wilson wanted to stock his new product in all of those establishments.

That Wilson's "delivery teams" comprised only him and Joe (and possibly one of his other stepsons) was not important. Perception is what mattered. That Rockport was on the verge of summer (it was noted in the same column that "Mr. Frank Amazeen's ice cream parlors are open for the season") was, on the other hand, especially important, given that bottlers did the majority of their business at that time of year.

In the words of one northern bottler at the time: "We have but three months in which to transact our business—practically only 2 months with the rainy days and the chilly days. In the south they can go all the time.

But in the winter, we have to rent out our horses for plowing the snow and things of that kind."

In some areas, business was already competitive. The Granite State Spring Water Company of Haverhill boasted of a "lively" business, bottling some twenty-one different brands and employing "upwards of 50 hands, 12 horses and four mules." But only ten miles up the road from their plant, in Lawrence, the Freedman Brothers Bottlers and Tonic Dealers was currently filing for bankruptcy, owing some $3,775 to creditors (the largest of which was none other than Gloucester's Merchant Box & Cooperage, which was owed $488).

Many beverages were still being marketed as "tonics" in the traditional sense. A sampling of ads from May 1907, the month Thomas Wilson's new bottling plant went online, show products such as "New Drink GLORIA—gives the vigour of youth. Half a day of new and vigorous life in every drink." Some of these beverages were specific remedies (laxative Bromo Quinine asserted, "There is only one Bromo Quinine!"), while others were more general ("If you need a tonic, ask your doctor for our non-alcoholic sarsaparilla").

Speaking of "tonic," this is probably a good point at which to pause and address this term. Twin Lights has always made tonic—not "soda" or "pop" or "cokes." In this part of the country, people drink tonic. The use of *tonic* as a byword for soda almost certainly originated in the same place as the soft drink itself: the pharmacies and apothecaries where carbonated water was first combined with mixtures of special ingredients that proffered some kind of curative or restorative health benefits ("a tonic for what ails you").

Its use never became widespread. *Soda* became the accepted term in most places, including in the Northeast. *Pop* is still common in the Midwest, while *coke* is still used in the South as a generic term for not just Coca-Cola but any flavor of soda. But in Greater Boston, the use of *tonic* has held firm for generations, especially to the north. It is fading, however. In a 2012 *Boston Globe* article, South Boston native Billy Baker suggested this was as much to do with age as geography, adding that the best available research shows that, at most, one in five Massachusetts residents still use the term *tonic*. But the place where the term *tonic* remains most prevalent, anywhere in the country (according to research by the website PopvsSoda), also happens to be Twin Lights territory: Essex and Middlesex Counties in Massachusetts.

When these "tonics" were not ascribing health properties (however specific or vague) to their consumption, they were being associated with indulgence and social activity. This was inherent in the soda fountain experience, where the social aspect was as important as the beverage itself. Now, increasingly, bottled soft drinks were being marketed as a product of leisure. An ad for Hood's, another brand of sarsaparilla, declared, "Spring is here—The Lazy Season," adding, "That peculiar lazy sensation is in the air." And what better place to enjoy "the lazy season" and a cold tonic than Rockport in the summertime?

Chapter 6

HOW TO MAKE A BOTTLE
OF TWIN LIGHTS TONIC

The machine that was set up in the back of Thomas Wilson & Co. Grocery was a basic apparatus. It was upright, with rubber tubes connected to it and room for only one bottle at a time. Hand and foot levers controlled the valves for syrup and carbonated water going into the bottle, and then the stopper was pulled into place. It was rudimentary and could get messy, but it worked.

Today inside the Twin Lights factory, it is quiet. There is a beautiful old combination safe in the corner of the office with hand-painted lettering on it in the company's signature shade of blue: "Thomas Wilson & Co.—Twin Lights Quality Beverages." Over the desk are some old framed photos— George Sears sitting in a Rockport Fire Department hook-and-ladder truck, Joe Sears with the volunteer fire crew in front of the Sandy Bay Engine House—all somewhat faded now from decades of sunlight coming in through the front window.

On the second floor is the syrup room. Access to this room is via a narrow and creaky flight of stairs. Pierce Sears, the eighty-eight-year-old current proprietor of Twin Lights, repeatedly warns his visitors to take it slowly and to be sure to hold on to something. There are a couple of steps that one could put their foot through should they try to go bounding back down them with too much urgency.

At the top of the stairs sits a thick wood workbench with an old cast-iron weighing scale affixed to it. Rarely used anymore, it dates to the early days of the company, but it's kept here for weighing out citric acid

Old combination safe with hand-painted lettering in the company's signature shade of blue. *Pierce Sears collection.*

powder, when needed, for flavoring. (Also called "sour salt," citric acid is a common additive that provides a tart, tangy taste in foods like candy and fruit-flavored soda.)

Few people outside of the immediate family have ventured up the stairs in recent decades. It is said that George Sears never allowed anyone up there, adding to its mystery. But Pierce insists it is not secret or anything, "it's just not very interesting." In the early years, this area would have been known as the laboratory. Up here, Thomas Wilson kept necessary items such as

Joe Sears on Ladder 1 at the old fire station in Dock Square next to the old police station in 1909. *Pierce Sears collection.*

weights, measures, beakers, thermometers, wall charts and various utensils, all critical to the tonic-making process.

In the nineteenth century, pharmacists, apothecaries and bottlers usually had to produce their own extracts, the source of flavor in a soft drink. It could be laborious and costly, and it involved placing—variously—fruits, roots, herbs and spices into a jar with alcohol and letting it steep for days, weeks or, sometimes, even months.

Very few continued making their own extracts into the twentieth century. For most, the availability of mass-produced pre-made extracts had removed this step from the average bottler's process. But they still had to do the second step, which involved blending the extract with a sugar-syrup mixture to create what is called the "simple syrup." The syrup can then be mixed with carbonated water to produce a soda. Eventually, this step, too, was eliminated for most. Today, most bottlers (and restaurants, convenience stores, etc.) purchase their syrup as a "post mix," which can be added directly to carbonated water. But not all do this. A few independent soda makers, like Pierce Sears, still create their own syrup. The biggest reason for this is that they use real cane sugar in their drinks (nearly all post mix today is made with high fructose corn syrup). Up in the syrup room is where this process (still) takes place. There are a pair of large, glass-lined, stainless-steel tanks, and the recipe, Pierce insists again, is hardly a secret. It is called "hot process," For the record, the following description is how it has always been done at Twin Lights.

"It's just a simple syrup recipe: nine gallons of water to one hundred pounds of sugar. That is what we use. I do not know what others do, but that

The stainless-steel tank in the syrup room holds the simple syrup, which is then transferred to the small tank where flavoring is added and piped downstairs to the filling machine. *Author's collection.*

has always been our recipe. It's heated slowly in a large tank and stirred by a big propeller like an outboard motor prop at the bottom of the tank and yields sixteen gallons." The large tank holds thirty-six gallons of finished simple syrup. Pierce never makes more than eighteen gallons of water with two hundred pounds of sugar.

From there, you move to the smaller tank for the next step: "Now, that's a big supply of simple syrup. So, from there you measure it out in gallons and add the extract for whichever flavor of tonic you are making. And then some citric acid, if needed for that particular flavor."

The citric acid comes in a large bag, in granulated powder form, and must first be processed in a separate container with very warm water (so it will dissolve more easily).

An often-asked question is, why is citric acid used in soft drinks? According to Pierce, its function is to add tartness especially to fruit sodas and colas. It provides a sharp, tangy taste and lengthens the shelf life as a preservative in beverages.

Pierce has never added caffeine to his soft drinks, having never seen the need to do so. In the 1950s, he said, his dad made a diet ginger ale that did not go well, and Pierce has since abandoned any diet sodas.

There is a set of filters, pipes and a pump that goes down into the floor and sends the syrup from this second tank, down through the ceiling, to the bottling machine on the floor below.

In the early days, before there was an upstairs in which to locate the syrup room, syrup had to be gravity-fed to the bottling machine. Syrup was placed in a large stone or tin-lined copper vessel with a spigot on the bottom, then placed on a high shelf or hoisted up by a pulley, with a tube running between the syrup jug and the machine. It was also vital to keep the area clean and containers tightly covered. The sweet liquid was a magnet for insects, flies and other matter that could clog valves, contaminate syrup and even ruin entire bottling runs. A "Syrup Spy Filter," marketed to bottlers at the time, was a small "window" device which could be inserted into the line of black rubber hose to monitor the liquid.

James W. Tufts, who made his fortune in the soda fountain business, penned one of the definitive publications of the era, *The Manufacture and Bottling of Carbonated Beverages* (1888). In it, he offered some quaint but essential advice regarding this step in the process:

> *When flavoring syrup, put in one ingredient at a time and mix thoroughly before adding another, using a wooden spatula or stick to stir. Never use metal. Use only the best flavors and coloring and beware of cheap dealers and fraudulent goods. Do not confound quality with strength. The essential qualities of bottlers' flavors are delicate fruitiness of flavor, rich aroma, and solubility. Too great concentration impairs these qualities and injures the bright, clear, sparkling appearance of the beverage. Coloring should be used very carefully. Avoid high colors.*

Ginger ale was Wilson's bestseller right out of the gate and remains perhaps Twin Lights' signature flavor today. It has remained probably its most unchanged recipe, too, says Pierce. To create the legendary Twin Lights Pale Dry Ginger Ale, a combination of ginger extracts was used. "Yes, a variety of two or three different ones," he smiles, without giving away too much. "A little bit of the Number 14 ginger extract, just so much of the Number 2…a little something like that."

Foote & Jenks was the main extract suppliers to the Twin Lights bottling company for over one hundred years. Company founders Charles E. Foote

The original offices of Foote & Jenks in Jackson, Michigan, from which Twin Lights bought its extract for over one hundred years. *Library of Congress.*

and Charles C. Jenks were pharmacists. On April 4, 1884, they opened a small drugstore at 216 Main Street, now West Michigan Avenue, in Jackson, Michigan.

In the back room, the duo experimented with fragrances to create a line of cosmetics, powders, lotions, sachets and perfumes. They hit it big with Linden Bloom, a fragrance captured from the flower of the linden tree. An 1889 newspaper edition, of the *Jackson Citizen Industrial* claimed that a bottle of the perfume "probably adorns every dresser in the city."

Advertised as "happy, sweet and pungent fine, pure as dew and picked as wine," Linden Bloom was a favorite of Frances Cleveland, wife of President Grover Cleveland, and Lily Langtry, a popular actress of the day. They gave testimonials for the fragrance, and Foote & Jenks soon found national and international demand for its products.

The key, they said in an advertisement at the time, was that Foote & Jenks products were "free from lead, arsenic, zinc, bismuth, mercury and other poisonous substances, which at an alarming degree are so generally employed by unscrupulous makers."

Experiments in the back room there to extract citrus fruit oils for use in their perfumes launched Foote and Jenks as pioneers in the manufacturing of flavorings. The process, which they kept secret, produced a quality product that was soon in demand by ice cream, candy, beverage and pharmaceutical makers.

By 1934, Foote & Jenks was one of only three companies in the country that manufactured bulk flavors exclusively. It had ten salesmen covering forty-eight states, and its products were shipped worldwide through the company's export department in New York City.

Innovation was key to the company's growth. It developed much of its own processing equipment and maintained a testing laboratory staffed by two chemists who ran tests on flavors and developed new extracts, some at the urging of big customers.

It soon became one of the six largest flavoring manufacturers among more than six hundred in the country. Its competitors called Foote & Jenks the "Tiffany of the industry."

If the failed introduction of "New Coke" in 1985 proved anything, it was that customers know what they like, and they do not want anyone changing it. Twin Lights was loyal to Foote & Jenks for most of its extracts, but there were exceptions, such as Twin Lights orange. Orange, another huge seller, was unique because it was made with a combination of fruit oils, fresh fruit and natural citric acid from the oranges. It was formulated by Sunkist Growers Cooperative, but the flavor that Pierce used to buy was nothing like today's Sunkist brand orange soft drink.

"I forget what the flavoring was called, 'California Orange' or something, but it was a liquid that came in boxes of six gallons each," remembers Pierce. "It was a pale orange liquid, with packets of additional coloring that you could add to it, depending on how orange you wanted it to be. But it was refrigerated because it had real orange in it. So, whenever we ordered it, we had to drive down to Providence, a ninety-six-mile trip, to the cold storage facility down there where it came in, to pick it up. We would get six-pack of one-gallon cans, and they had to stay refrigerated. But each gallon would make quite a few cases."

It was also Pierce's personal favorite flavor of all time—until it disappeared. "Around 1988–89, suddenly, with no warning at all, it became unavailable. You just could not get it anymore. I do not know why they stopped it. It was so wonderful. You cannot imagine how wonderful it was! I grew up on it and, well, I've never tasted something to its equal."

We surmise that Sunkist Growers decided to no longer make its concentrate available to small independent bottlers like Twin Lights. The company had introduced Sunkist soft drinks nationally in 1979. By 1988, the product had become the largest-selling orange drink by being franchised to the two largest national soft drink bottler networks, Coke and Pepsi bottlers, gaining instant national distribution.

Twin Lights did try to find a replacement, including one that came in a five-gallon pale from Chicago. "It was horrible," say Pierce flatly. "So, my father went and got a few different extracts from different places and conjured up his own little mixture that he was happy with. But it did not compare. And people noticed the difference. I know because I was one of them! People were really disappointed, and we actually lost business because of that."

"I still have gallon containers of different syrups sitting out there, like birch beer, which is a clear tonic, that I just can't use, because they did not work for us," Pierce sighs. "I know other bottlers that use that particular syrup, for instance, and their customers love it. But, for me, it just did not compare with our birch beer. So, there it sits."

As Thomas Wilson and Joe Sears grew the business, the flavors they produced—in addition to ginger ale and orange—included root beer, birch beer, sarsaparilla, cream soda, strawberry, lemon-lime, grape, punch, cola, half-and-half, Tom Collins, quinine, golden ginger ale and, of course, plain soda water. Certain "fresh" flavorings that could be served at a fountain, such as those made from cream or fresh fruits, were not really an option for bottlers yet.

Even more so than flavorings, the quality of water to which a bottler had access was crucial. For one thing, it is the single most prominent ingredient in a bottle of tonic. Many bottlers founded their operations on top of a gurgling spring. Polar Beverages began this way. Chelmsford's popular ginger ale originally came from the Chelmsford Spring Company, and Walker's Famous Beverages were a product of the Middlesex Fells Spring in Melrose. Simpson Spring Company in Easton, Massachusetts, founded in the late 1800s, is still bottling craft sodas with water from its factory's adjacent spring.

Bottlers without access to a pure spring were sometimes forced to rely on archaic, yet elaborate, filtration systems, which involved filling the inside of a barrel with layers of sand, charcoal and/or burlap through which to filter water to remove sediment or impurities.

Luckily for Thomas Wilson, Rockport had a wonderful source of local water via Cape Pond provided by the town's water authority and still in use today (which means the water in Twin Lights beverages has also remained constant). In 1909, his annual bill for this water came to ten dollars. By comparison, the

Turk's Head Inn that year had a water bill of nearly ten times that amount, around ninety-five dollars. Still, a good value for Rockport water.

Ice was also crucial to the soft drink manufacturing process.

The George H. Todd Company, purveyors of ice and coal, would come by in the morning with their horse teams to deliver vast amounts of ice. There were no refrigeration units in those days (but the water needed to be cold!), so a large wooden trough in the basement with pipes running along the bottom would be filled up with ice. They would deliver up to one hundred pounds each day, which was loaded through a window at ground level that opened into the basement. Todd probably bought his ice from Cape Pond Ice Company.

Cape Pond Ice Company was started in Gloucester in 1848 by blacksmith Nathaniel R. Webster, who recognized the need for supplying the fresh fish industry with a reliable, volume source of ice. Prior to that time, fish—primarily halibut and cod—was preserved by salting and brine.

Webster dammed a local brook and built his first icehouse on what became known as Webster's Pond, today the site of Veteran's Memorial School and the Route 128 extension.

The ice industry went through rapid growth, and within four years, Webster built icehouses on Upper- and Lower-Day's Ponds, where Foster's Service Station is located, and on Cape Pond in Rockport, which the company is still named after.

Webster's son took over the Cape Ann ice monopoly in 1858. Two of the company icehouses, which burned in the 1940s, were known as the "Great House" and the "Grove." Today, only massive granite foundations remain. Cape Pond remains the primary water supply for the town of Rockport.

As the fisheries flourished in the years following the Civil War, so did the ice industry. Every body of water accessible by teams of men and horses was soon harvested for ice during winter months. The "frozen lode" was stored in salt marsh hay, cork and sawdust insulation until it was needed in the summer. Competitors also entered the local ice industry—most prominently Francis W. Homans, who, in 1876, created a thirty-two-acre man-made lake on Essex Avenue for the purpose of harvesting ice. His house at Fernwood Lake in West Gloucester was at the time the largest building in Massachusetts, measuring 105 feet by 205 feet, and capable of holding ten thousand tons of ice.

After a lively period of "ice wars," when the two competing businesses reportedly sabotaged each other's winter harvests, in 1908, the Cape Pond Ice and Fernwood Lake companies merged.

Ice was delivered daily to Wilson and used to keep the water super cooled to make the carbonation better. *Library of Congress.*

The industry employed large crews of men to harvest, store and deliver ice around Cape Ann. In 1916, sixty men were employed during the cutting season, with twenty teams and five automobile trucks. In addition to a large, delivered household ice trade, the Cape Pond Ice Company continued to supply large quantities of ice to the Gloucester fisheries, and also to the summer hotels, restaurants, bars, soda fountains, drugstores and local beachside businesses like Jimmy's Sunrise near Front Beach.

Nathaniel Webster dammed a local brook and named it Webster's Pond. Ice was harvested each winter. *Cape Pond Ice website.*

In the early 1940s, Gloucester Cold Storage was constructed on the Gloucester waterfront on the new State Fish Pier. The new plant took advantage of modern mechanical refrigeration technology, using electricity instead of relying on Mother Nature during New England winters and cutting ice from the ponds.

In 1946, entrepreneur John Ryan built the present Cape Pond Ice manufacturing plant at the end of Commercial Street, on the site of the Fort Wharf Company on Gloucester Harbor. This was a "modern" block plant, with 3,600 four-by-two-by-one-foot molds for three-hundred-pound ice blocks, manufactured in an indoor concrete "pond" refrigerated with compressed ammonia and harvested by overhead cranes. Over three hundred tons of ice could be made each day to reliably serve the needs of a flourishing fishing industry.

Cape Pond Ice Company still exists with the ad slogan "The Coolest Guys Around."

Today, ice and water continue to be essential to the making and consuming of soft drinks.

Next, the water had to be carbonated. Among the confluence of developments making the bottling trade more accessible around the time Twin

Lights began was the arrival of liquefied carbon dioxide, a vast improvement on previous methods, such as combining sulfuric acid and marble dust (aka calcium carbonate) and then forcing the gas into a pressurized cylinder filled with water. This early process of "charging the water" was tedious, stinky and sometimes dangerous. But now there were at least a dozen firms producing a liquefied solution, rendering older methods obsolete.

In addition to using super-cold water when carbonating (because it absorbs the carbonation better that way), Pierce says Twin Lights has never been shy about how much CO2 it uses. It is one of the reasons its beverages taste as crisp as they do. "It just provides a little zip on the tongue," he explains. "I'm always surprised by how little gas other bottlers use. We always put plenty of CO2 in our tonic—especially the ginger ale. There's nothing worse than a flat ginger ale."

Next, when it is time to bottle, you need…bottles. Throughout the 1800s, the glass containers used by bottlers would have been mouth- or hand-blown. Despite the use of molds, and, later, the glass-blowing process becoming semi-automated in the latter part of the 1800s, it was still an imperfect art. No two bottles were ever perfectly identical. Everything changed in 1903, when Michael J. Owens, a self-taught American inventor, unveiled the world's first completely automatic glass-forming machine. It introduced an automated process that could create, time after time, perfectly identical, uniformly shaped glass containers—and at a consistently greater speed. Not only would this make bottles more affordable, but the perfect consistency also meant that the long-wrestled-with problem of creating a reliable leak-proof seal was now infinitely more solvable. By 1910, the new machines could produce over 57,000 a day, a big increase over the 1,500 a day produced by hand-blowing a few years earlier.

While this was a remarkable innovation—indeed, one we still use today (consider our everyday use of bottles for foods, liquids and medicines)—the transition to these machine-made bottles was not immediate. Instead, it was drawn out over nearly two decades between 1900 and 1920. This was largely due to Owens's machine's initial price tag. But there was also something of a revolt by workers in the factories. Obviously, if your labor skill is bottle-blowing, the last thing you wanted was a machine doing your job. But by 1920, the transition was pretty much complete.

And that brings us to the next step in the process: capping and corking. While the bottle cap might seem insignificant today, it was a profoundly transformative development in the history of the soft drink industry, for reasons that include efficiency, hygiene and preservation of product.

Michael J. Owens stands in front of his automatic glass-bottle-forming machine in 1910. His machine could make 240 bottles per minute. *Investor's Weekly Magazine.*

As previously mentioned, it was nearly impossible in the mid-nineteenth century to keep carbonated water fizzy for very long. In the latter half of the 1800s, countless inventors (as in, hundreds and possibly even thousands of them, from Lowell, Massachusetts, to Dublin, Ireland) applied for patents for various bottle closure ideas. None of the existing options were guaranteed to retain a tight seal (which ran the risk of turning their contents rancid or, worse, toxic). It was the quest of the age, like a nineteenth-century space race, to figure out the best solution—one that was reliable, affordable and easy to affix. One inventor in Chicago boasted that his "Stopper Injector" system would enable "a mere boy" to affix stoppers in soft drink bottles "twice as fast as two men" (child labor laws were just on the horizon).

During this period, a variety of stopper solutions would emerge as market leaders for a time before being replaced by another new idea. These included wire cork stoppers (like those found on a champagne bottle), the Putnam Swing Stopper (1859–1905; akin to what you might find today on a German or Belgian beer bottle), the Codd or ball stopper

The Putnam Swing Stopper (1859–1905) was used mostly on beer bottles. It was a wire stop with a rubber seal pushed down with a ceramic stopper. *American Bottler Magazine.*

(in which a rubber ball or marble sat within the neck of a specially designed bottle) and the Hutchinson Patent Spring Stopper.

This latter option became the closure of choice by the late 1800s and remained so until at least 1910 (as bottle-making slowly changed over to Owens's machines). Like most bottlers at the time, this is the system that Thomas Wilson would use for the first few years of business. It sealed the bottle inside, at the neck, with a rubber disc. Attached to the disk was a metal coil that would be used to pull the rubber disc up against the neck to seal the bottle, once filled. When one was ready to drink the contents, they would simply push the stopper back down into the bottle, opening the neck up for the liquid to flow out and leaving the stopper inside. It was not terribly hygienic. It is also sometimes credited for the origin of the term *soda pop* (the Hutchinson stopper made a "pop" sound when opened), but this is a topic of much conjecture.

But the "crown cork" was about to change everything.

An Irish-born immigrant named William Painter came to America in 1858 at the age of twenty and embarked on a life as an inventor. Among his inventions was a device for detecting counterfeit money, a safety ejection seat for train passengers and a paper-folding machine. None of these, nor any of the other eighty-odd patents he secured over the course of his lifetime, made him rich. But in 1891, he introduced the crown bottle cap, which he so named, the story goes, because it gave "a crowning and beautiful effect to the bottle."

Initially dubbed "crown corks," the metal discs were lined with a thin layer of cork to prevent the metal cap from encountering the liquid once affixed over the top of the bottle. Later crowns would be lined with rubber, then plastic. Eventually—much to Pierce Sears's dismay—crowns were reduced to cheap, lightweight metal with no lining at all, which is what most bottles use today.

The basic function remains unchanged, however, with the cap's corrugated edge being pressed around the rim of a bottle to create a completely leak-proof seal. Coincidentally, Painter also patented a "bottle cap lifter" (aka

Opposite, top: Drawing of the Hutchinson Patent Spring Stopper, first used by Thomas Wilson in 1910. *Author's collection*.

Opposite, bottom: A 1901 ad in *American Bottler* by Standard Crown and Cork for its line of crown stoppers. *American Bottler Magazine*.

Right: The first early crown version had the Twin Lights logo and the flavor indicated. Later versions listed only the flavor. *Author's collection*.

bottle opener) that same year for removing his crown caps. Then, to further aid in the adoption of his new product, he also invented a foot-powered "crowner" for bottlers to use. Because his crown caps really needed the perfect uniformity of Owens's machine-made bottles to work best, the transition from Hutchinson Stoppers to Painter's crown caps was a gradual one. But by about 1915, the Hutchinson Stopper was considered obsolete. Painter would die a wealthy man. The company he founded, Crown Cork & Seal, is today an $8 billion business. It remains widely held that, while the screw-top cap is the most significant closure invention of the last century, the crown cap is surely an undisputed second.

Another reason for the gradual transition to crown caps might have been that it was somewhat costly for bottlers. But this did not seem to deter Thomas Wilson, as he appears to have made the switch by about 1910 or 1911.

Once a bottle is filled and capped, it gets turned upside-down once or twice to ensure the syrup and carbonated water blend (a practice still done today with every bottle of Twin Lights, as it also provides a quick visual safety check for impurities). The bottles then needed to be labeled. It is uncertain when Wilson began using labels or how often he used them in the early years. The only evidence of their labeling efforts in the first couple of decades is an antiquated foot-powered labeling machine that sat for many years in the back corner of the factory, gathering dust. Made by the Economic Machine Company of Worcester, Massachusetts, it would have cost about $100 at the time. It could label up to forty-eight bottles per minute using a foot lever attached to a heavy coil spring. "As fast as any operator can handle the bottles," stated the ads. In practice, the machine was imperfect—prone to tearing and skipping labels—but it saved labeling by hand, a task that would have fallen to poor Joe Sears, who would have

Pierce turns over each bottle, mixing the flavor and checking the color as each leaves the Dixie filler/bottle-capper machine. *Author's collection.*

Labeling machines
came in foot-
powered or electric
power versions from
Economic Machine
Company. *American
Bottler Magazine.*

had to make a paste out of rye flour and hot water, then swipe the back of the label across a "gummer" to apply the paste before finally affixing it to the bottle by hand.

In 1879, William LePage began manufacturing "fish glue" in Rockport with fish skins, bones and cartilage. It was called "Russian belting cement," as it was used to glue leather belting together. Eventually, he changed the name of the company to Russian Cement Company. In 1881, he moved his factory to Gloucester and developed a full line of glues, adhesives and other products with the LePage brand. What better place to find a supply of fish skins and parts than America's number-one fishing port in Gloucester? The accompanying image is an ad for LePage's label paste found in the 1902 edition of *American Bottler Magazine*. This was another

Three of the paper flavor labels, including Pale Dry Ginger Ale, Orange, Lemon-Lime, and three generic Beverage labels for clear bottles using flavor designation crowns. *Pierce Sears collection*.

An ad of the Russian Cement Company in Gloucester, Massachusetts, for its Le Pages label paste. Joe Sears used to make his own paste. *American Bottler Magazine*.

local Gloucester company that may have supplied the Wilson Bottling Company for many years.

All bottles were returnable. Customers paid a deposit, and bottles were returned and refilled. Cases of empty bottles were picked up as new cases were delivered, and these empty bottles then needed to be washed and refilled. In the early days, rinsing the empty bottles in a sink would have sufficed. But the Pure Food and Drug Act of 1906 changed that. Suddenly, food and beverage producers were accountable to a new set of consumer protection regulations that were being strictly enforced by the U.S. government. By the time Wilson launched his company, there was a process in place for adequately cleaning bottles. (The role of "bottle washer" was indeed a real job title.)

The cleaning process included a soaking and rinsing step. In between these steps, a person would scrub the bottle with an automated bottle-cleaning machine. This machine would insert a bristled brush that would rotate inside the bottle. To rinse, a spindle device was attached to the sink that would send jets of water inside multiple bottles at a time, and they would be left upside-down to dry. Then, the whole process would begin again.

A remarkable confluence of events and innovations combined to spark the bottling revolution that occurred in the early 1900s. Innovation was truly speeding along. For the first time in their lives, people were experiencing things like electrical power and wireless radio and witnessing the automation of countless once-manual tasks. On top of that, you could now get refreshing bubbly water, just like it came out of a natural spring, delivered to your door in a bottle, with the flavor of sweet Jamaican ginger in it. What a time to be alive!

Chapter 7

WE'RE IN BUSINESS (1910-1920)

T homas Wilson's bottled tonics were a hit around Rockport almost out of the gate. In almost no time, Thomas Wilson & Company had outgrown its small space in the back of the grocery store, and work began on a new building next door, on the Wilson's property. (Today, that building is 69 Broadway and still houses the Twin Lights plant.) Soon, there was a new structure with green wood shingles, fresh white paint on the trim and front door and a large sign over that door that stretched the entire width of the front of the building. It read:

THOMAS WILSON & Co.
HIGH GRADE CARBONATED BEVERAGES

Unfortunately, the sign has been lost to time, according to Pierce. He wishes he still had it as a memento and a piece of Rockport history. Today, the factory is painted white and still retains the picture window by which passersby can watch the filling line from the driveway. At first glance, the structure looks like a private residence instead of a soft drink bottling factory. I remember as a schoolkid going on a class trip to the Coca-Cola Bottling Company on Memorial Drive in Cambridge to see the entire operation from a sidewalk next to the building on Storrow Drive. Thousands of green "hobble skirt"–shaped Coke bottles would zoom by, fed from a back room somewhere and go through the filling and capping machine to be put in the yellow and red Coca-Cola cases and into the warehouse.

The factory as it looks today with the picture window through which passersby can watch the bottles being filled. *Author's collection.*

The original Thomas Wilson & Co. factory sign of 1910 after the name was changed from Consolidated Bottling Works. *Pierce Sears collection.*

Thomas Wilson & Company was a perfectly adequate name for a bottling works. But it needed a better brand name for its soft drinks. Wilson's old mentor at American Seltzer in Beverly, for example, had since branded his products Garden City Beverages, while George A. Davis in Gloucester was adopting the name Royal Club for his.

So, what to call Rockport's local tonic? For Thomas Wilson and Joe Sears, the answer was obvious. In fact, it was sitting just three-fourths of a mile offshore on Thacher Island, that tiny, rocky tract of land in the Atlantic Ocean just beyond Loblolly Cove. Thacher Island is home to the Cape Ann Light Station, which operates an iconic pair of lighthouses known as the "twin lights." In his 1894 travel guide, *The North Shore of Massachusetts Bay, An Illustrated Guide*, Benjamin D. Hill writes: "A drive through the village and out Mt. Pleasant Street brings us very near to Straitsmouth Island and light, at the entrance to Rockport harbor, and to the famous lighthouses on Thacher's Island, those familiar beacons, like sturdy sentinels, standing guard for Cape Ann."

The famous lighthouses date to 1771, when the colonial government purchased the island from its then-owner to commission a light station on the property. John Hancock was instrumental in having two lighthouses

The Twin Lights from a 1900 photo showing the two 125-foot granite towers, fog signal, covered walkways and two keeper houses on the left. *Author's collection.*

built. Hancock had significant shipping interests, owning many coastal and Europe-bound ships. He petitioned the Massachusetts General Court to have them built on Thacher Island. The reason he asked for two was to enable seamen, especially those coming from Europe, to distinguish these twin lights from the single light to the south, Boston Light, and the single light to the north, Portsmouth Harbor light. In those early days, there was not the ability to provide blinking lights as is the case today (called characteristics, each lighthouse having its own blinking pattern), so two were needed. Their light beams reached out twenty-two miles to sea with the newly installed First Order Fresnel lens in each tower. These lighthouses were also the first to mark a dangerous spot in the ocean; all others at the time simply marked harbor entrances. In 1861, two new towers, constructed of granite and stretching to 166 feet above sea level, were completed. It is these iconic lighthouses that still exist today and that adorn every bottle of Twin Lights Tonic. When a new town seal for Rockport was adopted in 1888, the "twin lights" was chosen to represent the town. Along with Motif Number 1, the famous red fish shack on Bradley Wharf, the twin lights have come to signify Rockport for residents and visitors alike. Today, Thacher Island, along with its sister Straitsmouth Island a mile northwest, attracts hundreds of visitors, who climb the towers, walk the trails and view the displays in the visitor centers. Pierce, we have two of your quart bottles on display if you need a couple.

Pierce says that the name was the natural choice, because Rockport has always been very proud of its twin lights. "Nowadays it's on everything here—fire department, police department, and all DPW vehicles—you see it everywhere." Indeed, you can also find it on the sign for nearby Bass Rocks Golf Club, Rockport's Educational Center and even the local Dunkin' Donuts. It also appears on the U.S. Coast Guard cutter *Maria Bray*. In the 1990s, when the USCG commissioned a new fleet of "Keeper class" ships (which would be named after famous lighthouse keepers and, fittingly, used for tending to coastal buoys and other navigation and safety-related tasks), they selected the wife of one-time Thacher Island Light keeper Alexander D. Bray for her heroic tending of the twin lights over several days in December 1864 while her husband was stranded ashore. In the summer of 2020, a new local brand of India pale ale, Twin Lights New England Double IPA, was introduced by Rockport Brewing Company. It is brewed and packaged by Riverwalk Brewing Company of Newburyport, Massachusetts. The artwork for the can was created by local artist Stefan Mierz, who owns the Art Nook Gallery on Bearskin Neck.

Top, left: The new Town of Rockport seal, adopted in 1888, features the Twin Lights. *Author's collection.*

Top, right: Twin Lights images used by Bass Rocks golf club, Rockport Educational Center, local Dunkin' Donuts and all Department of Public Works town equipment. *Author's collection.*

Bottom: A newly introduced local beer is called Twin Lights New England Double IPA. *Author's collection.*

It's uncertain where the original artwork came from for the label. (Pierce believes it may have been designed by someone in-house at the printworks company from which they ordered their labels.) But it was a symbol that resonated with both Thomas Wilson and Joe Sears. Their fathers were both mariners and fishermen (and Joe Sears's father, of course, had even died at sea), and the ocean was a part of their heritage—just like Rockport, the town in which they were both born. These twin lights were very personal to each man, having guided their fathers safely home for many years. At one time, over 70,000 vessels passed by Thacher annually in the mid-1800s. These lights have been important to mariners' safety for over two hundred years.

Pierce has been very generous to the townspeople as well as to the Thacher Island Association. A few years ago, two friends, John Salisbury and Phil Hopkins, came to Pierce with an idea to make up Twin Lights T-shirts using the various bottle label artwork designs and donating the proceeds of the sales to the association. This has been a very successful annual operation, resulting in significant funds for the restoration and maintenance efforts of the association. Pierce was never a proponent of advertising per se but felt this idea was just right for him to help maintain and preserve the twin lights, whose image is iconic around Cape Ann.

BUSINESS GREW STEADILY. PEOPLE were head over heels for tonic, and at four cents a bottle, it had become an even cheaper beverage option than tea or coffee at the time. The big seller for Twin Lights was its ginger ale. This was not unusual—ginger ale was by far the most popular flavor around the country at this point. Coca-Cola was working on changing that, of course. But for Twin Lights, ginger ale would remain its signature flavor, even today.

As for Coke, it had grown from 120 bottling plants around the country in 1904 to 400 plants in 1910. By 1919, the company was up to 1,200. Coca-Cola was being built atop a foundation of small, family-owned operations, just like Thomas Wilson's. It was around this time that a Coca-Cola rep paid a visit to Rockport. He pitched Thomas Wilson on becoming a Coke bottler, offering him a franchise. Wilson declined.

"Coke made people millionaires," says Pierce. "Many small family bottlers who became early Coke franchisees became millionaires. Who knows what would have happened if we had gone that route?"

Nobody knows for sure why Wilson declined Coke's offer. However, Coke then was not yet the Coke we know now. Furthermore, the agreement likely limited his ability to produce other products, such as his own Twin Lights brand. We will never know, but it is possible that some degree of independent spirit and local pride played a part in his decision.

THE COUNTRY WAS SLOWLY transitioning from the horse age to the motorized age. On Main Street in Rockport, there were trolley tracks, motorized cars and horse-drawn delivery wagons, all sharing space on the busy dirt thoroughfare.

Thomas Wilson was still delivering via horse-drawn wagon, at least for now. A simple wagon then was simple to make and relatively affordable— under $100 (about $1,000 in today's money). But a stylish wagon was key for any worthwhile business enterprise. After all, your wagon was your greatest billboard, one you hauled around town on deliveries and parked out in front of your factory. Thomas Wilson's delivery wagon proudly displayed the company name along the side and could hold up to thirty cases. His horses were looked after by an Irishman named Timothy Sheahan Jr. who maintained a horse stable just down the road from the Twin Lights plant, on the corner of Broadway and School Street.

Their grocery store had been sold (to the Paradis family, which continued to run it for much of the twentieth century) so that Thomas Wilson and Joe Sears could focus full-time on their expanding bottleworks.

A postcard showing downtown upper Main Street in Rockport with trolley tracks, horse-drawn wagons and automobiles, circa 1900. *Sandy Bay Historical Society*.

Thomas Wilson's original grocery store wagon, soon converted to a soft drink wagon. *Pierce Sears collection.*

More new bottles arrived via railroad and were picked up at the depot. This meant that more new wood cases were needed. These were always ordered from Merchant Box & Cooperage in Gloucester, which was also benefiting from the bottling boom—it had now become the largest manufacturer of bottle cases in New England and was beginning to advertise nationally. The company was run at the time by Benjamin Smith and, later, his son Ben Smith II. The younger Smith, famously, was roommates with John F. Kennedy at Harvard. Years later, when JFK was elected president, he tapped Ben to serve out his term in the U.S. Senate. Afterward, Ben returned to running Merchant, and the Searses continued to order their boxes from him. (When Pierce was a kid, in the early 1940s, he would be assigned to shellac the new wood cases when they came in and was paid thirty-five cents an hour by his grandfather. "That was my first job here, when I was nine or ten," he explains. "I wasn't old enough to drive yet. But I was old enough to hold a paint brush.")

In 1919, George Sears, now age thirteen, somehow was old enough to drive already. That summer, he began working as a private driver for a wealthy summer resident (Dr. O'Connor of Watertown) who had a summer home in town near Front Beach. On the 1920 U.S. census, he even made his father, Joe Sears, list his profession as "chauffeur." George was obsessed with cars growing up, as was his brother (who would run a garage down the

Left: An advertisement for Merchant Box Company of Gloucester, which supplied wood cases to Thomas Wilson Bottling Company. *American Bottler Magazine*.

Below: A new Model T pickup truck with George Sears standing next to it, circa 1928. *Pierce Sears collection*.

street for a few years before going off to war). On two separate occasions when the town of Rockport ordered a new ambulance, George went down to Arkansas to pick it up and drive it back. He loved driving.

And George was not the only one driving now. Twin Lights was about to purchase its first motorized vehicle: a Ford Model T delivery truck. Not only was it the perfect way to mark the company's first decade in business; also, more crucially, it had survived what was a particularly tough period for bottlers during World War I.

For the previous thirty years, since the late 1800s, the price for a bottle of soda had held steady at "5 cents for small, 10 cents for large." But between 1914 and 1917, the cost of bottles (despite automation) increased 125 percent. The cost of labels and printed matter increased 25–50 percent, and caps and "tin ware" increased 25–40 percent. Meanwhile, suppliers were, in many cases, demanding cash payment from bottlers now. Previously, bottlers had been permitted one to two months' credit.

Worst of all, the cost of sugar more than doubled, from three and three-fourths cents per pound to nine cents per pound, and the government was readying to add an additional one-cent tax on top of that. As part of "Revenue to Defray War Expenses," Uncle Sam's effort to replenish the country's coffers after World War I, several taxes were proposed that would hit bottlers hard. These included a 10 percent tax on syrup, two cents per gallon on prepared (carbonated) waters and one cent per gallon on natural mineral waters. To top it off, in what the bottlers called "an utterly outrageous tax," Congress was preparing to place a levy on the storage of gas in CO_2 drums, which would more than double the cost to bottlers, from five cents to thirteen cents per pound.

Andrew P. Doyle of the Eastern Bottler Association of Massachusetts went before Congress representing a group of more than two hundred independent New England bottlers. In a remarkable exchange with lawmakers, he argued that most bottlers, in solidarity with the war effort, would settle for just breaking even for the next year, even two, but that the amounts being proposed would crush them. "The small manufacturers are willing to do everything they can and be patriotic," he told Congress. "We realize what we have got to do. We are willing to pay. If [breaking even] were the case, we would give three loud cheers and say everything was alright."

But, he continued, these taxes would put most of them out of business. He explained to Congress that the independent bottlers were the "little fellows" and "couldn't afford high-priced lawyers to present their case" like the big companies.

"I have got every dollar I have in the world invested in this business," Doyle continued. "Not only that, 95% of the stuff that is bottled by the people in our line of business is sold to working people."

He further laid out exactly how this would destroy the independent bottling industry. Wealthier bottlers, he said, would simply purchase the equipment (generators) needed to go back to the old-fashioned way of self-producing the gas (that is, "charging the water"), thereby dodging the tax on CO_2 canisters, while poorer bottlers that could not swing the capital expenditure for that equipment would be stuck paying it. "Within a year, more than 50% would be bankrupt and it will create a monopoly where two or three companies control the bulk of the business," he concluded.

In what was a momentous victory for independent bottlers, Congress agreed and waived the tax.

WITH PROHIBITION TAKING EFFECT on January 17, 1920, the next decade began with many beer brewers faced with finding an alternative product to make. "Cereal beverages" had been around for a decade or two. They were effectively low- or non-alcohol beer (this is when the term *near-beer* was coined). Brewers switching to near-beer were hard-pressed to find selling points for it, except that it was cold, quenched your thirst and, they suggested, could even go well with certain foods that don't pair well with sugary soda, "like cheese or oysters."

Many brewers simply pivoted to soft drinks. Bunker Hill Brewery, founded in the Boston neighborhood of Charlestown in 1821, had been making beer and ale for a century before Prohibition forced it into the soft drink business. Similarly, Polar Beverages was born after the original company had to give up making whiskey and focus on ginger ale and spring water.

Rockport had always been a dry town, so Prohibition did not impact sales close to home very much. But Twin Lights had developed a considerable business stocking the saloons of Gloucester, so it took a small hit there. Although, ginger ale, among other soft drinks, remained popular mixers for bootleg alcohol, so who knows what Twin Lights Tonic was being used for after it was delivered?

One of those saloons belonged to a famous Gloucester fisherman by the name of Howard Blackburn (1859–1932). Blackburn had been lost in the fog while fishing from his dory on the Grand Banks with his dory mate. His fishing schooner, *Grace L. Fears*, lost track of him during a severe snowstorm, so he rowed many miles to shore in below-freezing weather. His crewmate

Front entrance to Blackburn Tavern as it looks today. Not much has changed since it opened in 1883. *Author's collection.*

gave up and did not survive by the second day. Blackburn rowed for five days without food, water or sleep. He made it to shore in Newfoundland. Blackburn let his hand freeze to the oars so he would not lose his grip. He lost all his fingers and several toes and both thumbs to the first joint, making it impossible to continue in the fishing trade. He returned to Gloucester a hero. With help from the townspeople, he was able to open a successful saloon in 1883.

He was not satisfied sitting in his bar, so he decided to sail single-handed across the Atlantic Ocean. This had been done before by Alfred "Centennial" Johnson in 1876 and Joshua Slocum in 1898, but for a man with no fingers it was an amazing accomplishment. He sailed in 1899 in the modified Gloucester fishing sloop *Great Western* and reached England after sixty-two days at sea. His Blackburn Tavern remains today at 289 Main Street in Gloucester.

A second saloon was opened on upper Main Street with the Blackburn name on the building and on the pub sign in 1900 before the land area around it had been filled in and the Atlantic tide from Gloucester Harbor would wash up behind the pub in what is now the parking lot. Forty years

Blackburn's second saloon on upper Main Street has operated as Halibut Point Bar and Restaurant for the past forty years. *Cape Ann Museum.*

ago, it was reopened as Halibut Point Restaurant and Pub, serving local fishermen and workers from Gorton's Fish factory next door. In June 2020, it finally closed its doors.

Twin Lights did have its first (and only) run-in with the law during this time, however, in 1925.

The artificial sweetener saccharin (a product derived from coal tar that is some three hundred times as sweet as sucrose) had been introduced as a somewhat revolutionary development in the early 1900s. This was before anyone thought about "diet" soft drinks—saccharin was merely a new alternative to sugar (with a taste that some consumers, most notably President Theodore Roosevelt, even preferred). But researchers at the U.S. Food and Drug Administration were not so sure. As part of the Pure Food and Drug Act, the FDA ultimately deemed saccharin an inferior product to sugar ("devoid of food value"). Therefore, foods using saccharin in place of sugar were considered to be "adulterated." While the product was still declared safe for consumption, its use in a product like soda simply had to be stated somewhere, either on the bottle cap or the label.

Saccharin came in soluble crystal or powder form from suppliers, and bottlers found it to be an acceptable (and cost-saving) substitute to offset their sugar use. However, states across the country were now testing for it regularly and would fine bottlers for "adulterating" their products if it was not listed as an ingredient. Despite its relative seclusion up in Rockport, Twin Lights was still not so isolated as to be out of reach of the long arm of the food inspectors. In the summer of 1925, the Massachusetts Department of Public Health collected hundreds of food and drug samples from around the state, testing everything from milk and butter to maple syrup, to canned shrimp. Hundreds of violations were uncovered, including twenty-two samples of "adulterated" soft drinks that failed to list saccharin on their labels. Several bottlers were cited, including the Essex Bottling Company of Ipswich with a whopping five violations. Also cited was Twin Lights. Inspectors found two samples to be "adulterated" with saccharin, leading to both Thomas Wilson and Joe Sears being convicted of "violating the food laws." For such a small operation, they probably didn't see the need to go back and have an entirely new set of caps and/or labels printed up (or maybe they were just using up the ones they had before ordering new ones). But, nevertheless, they went to court and paid their fine (roughly fifty dollars, a not inconsiderable amount of money in those days). They also decided to stick to real sugar from that point on.

The Roaring Twenties were proving an interesting time. Pepsi was emerging out of a 1923 bankruptcy, while Coke was distancing itself from the pack. A decade earlier, in 1916, it had introduced its signature swirl "hoop skirt"–shaped bottle to differentiate the product from competitors. (Even reaching into a chest of ice, you would know when you grabbed a Coke bottle.) And in the 1920s, Coke was waging an unprecedented advertising campaign, including print, billboards and the use of celebrity spokespersons. It is interesting to note that Twin Lights never advertised after the first couple years of business. No radio, no TV, no print—nothing but the occasional Twin Lights logo on a promotional pen or calendar.

As the 1920s ended, the number of bottlers operating in Massachusetts was at its peak. But the next decade was going to have something to say about that.

Chapter 8

A DEPRESSION AND A WAR (1930–1945)

The 1930s and 1940s was a transitional time for Twin Lights. The period would begin with the death of one founder and conclude with the death of the other. In between, there was the company's first (and only) acquisition, the birth of Twin Lights' last living successor and, of course, the small matters of the Great Depression and World War II.

Beginning in 1929 with the October crash of the stock market, economies around the globe began to plummet severely, and America was hit hard. Next door in Gloucester, the fishing industry struggled; even closer to home in Rockport, the once-bustling granite quarries were seeing demand wind down. The Roaring Twenties had been a boom time for bottlers, but that was about to come to an end. So, too, was Thomas Wilson's stewardship of the company.

In the summer of 1932, Wilson died at age seventy-one. He had worked right up to the end of his life, living on the property and continuing to oversee the operation he'd built from the large house next door. He and cofounder Joe Sears both knew the business inside and out, and any passing of the torch from Thomas to Joe at this point would have been all but ceremonial.

Poetically, only a few weeks after losing his stepfather and mentor, Joe Sears would welcome his first grandson into the world. Twin Lights' current owner and operator, Pierce Sears, was born on September 28, 1932, to George and Gretchen Sears.

Pierce was born in and has always lived in Rockport. He was educated in Rockport schools, went to a small one-room schoolhouse on Broadway for kindergarten and the new George J. Tarr elementary school. He became interested in cameras, especially movie cameras. His mother gave him his first eight-millimeter movie camera in 1953, just before he left for basic training in the army. By 1960, he had acquired the top of the line, a Bolex movie camera. He has taken thousands of feet of footage around Rockport for all these years. Parades, fireworks, special events, fishing boats, his friends and his target shooting contests were just a few of his subjects. When he went off to the army after being drafted in 1952, he took his movie camera and recorded many of his experiences in Alaska. Prior to joining, he had attended Bentley College for two years (1952–54) and went off in 1954 to Military Police School in Georgia at Fort Gordon. The school was transferred to Fort McClellan in Alabama in 1975. Many of his fellow recruits' class of 212 were eventually based in the Canal Zone and in Alaska. It took him four months to complete basic training instead of the usual two, because of his knee injury from his truck wreck in 1949 that severely slowed him down. (See chapter 9.) Finally, he was put on a series of trains, ships and buses and ended up posted in a place called Delta Junction one hundred miles south of Fairbanks at Fort Greely. Delta Junction had a population of fewer than four hundred. It was the last town connected to the Alaskan Highway (Alcan), which connected the contiguous United States with Alaska.

Upon his discharge, he came back to Rockport to help his dad operate Twin Lights Beverages. In the early 1960s, he took up target shooting. He had a .22-caliber pistol and a .22 long rifle his grandfather had given him. He used them weekly at the range in a gravel pit at the end of Poole's Lane in Rockport. He joined the Rockport Sportsman's Club, which had its clubhouse in the Redmen's Hall near Front Beach. He also joined the Gloucester Indoor Range and began trap- and skeet shooting outdoors, usually on Sundays. Pierce said that he often carried his pistol under the front seat of his delivery truck so he could go directly to either shooting venue without having to go back home. The issue of guns in schools and school shootings in recent years has Pierce reminiscing that he delivered to schools that had many vending machines with a gun in his truck and is glad that he does not have to deliver to schools today. He moved into his grandmother's home after her death in 1960, after his father totally restored the inside of the 1920s home. He lives very comfortably there today at 71 Broadway, next to the factory. He has had most of his vast collection of movies transferred to DVD and has a sixty-inch TV he can watch them on.

Pierce was also a big boxing and wrestling fan. He has photographs taken with Rocky Marciano and Jack Dempsey and a variety of famous wrestlers.

Pierce (*back row, second from right*) at age three with his kindergarten class. His one-room schoolhouse was on Broadway. *Pierce Sears collection.*

One of his biggest thrills was to end up with his graven image on the front page of the August 18, 1997 issue of the *Wall Street Journal*. The story appeared on the top middle column and told of him and Twin Lights Beverages. The headline read, "Recipe for Nostalgia: Making Up Batches of Twin Lights Soda." His father, George, was active in the stock market and subscribed to the *Journal* regularly for years. Pierce often said that his father would have been proud to see him and their company honored there.

The two life events—Wilson's death and Pierce's birth?—triggered a series of personal changes for the Twin Lights family. Joe Sears moved his family out of their home on Jewett Street and into the large house at 71 Broadway, where his (now twice-widowed) mother, Mary, would remain, and from where he could oversee the operation next door, much as his stepfather, Thomas Wilson, had done.

Joe's son George, who had been residing with his wife and newborn son in the same (quite busy) home on Jewett Street with his parents, would move his family into a house at 1 Granite Street, which he purchased from his mother-in-law, Catherine Daily. (Her husband, Pearce Daily, was an Irish immigrant and a brakeman on the steam trains who had recently passed away, so she was happy to pass the home to her daughter and son-in-law at this point.) The house is located at the corner of Granite and King Streets, where, in the center of the intersection, there still stands an old granite watering trough and wood pump from the days when the road was traversed by horse and carriage. This is the house in which Pierce Sears would spend his childhood. It was a short five-minute walk down Railroad Avenue to the Twin Lights factory on Broadway, a trip he would make frequently, sometimes several times a day, over the next eighteen years.

His father's role at Twin Lights, meanwhile, was expanding rapidly. Now in his twenties, George had spent his whole life up to that point in the small plant. He loved the place and had decided early on that he wanted to take it over from his father one day. To that end, George was the first member of his family to enroll in college, choosing to study business and accounting. In the 1920s, Joe Sears had already given over the running of the syrup room to his son, and by the time Thomas Wilson died in 1932, George was confidently starting to handle much of the bookkeeping side of the business, too.

OUTSIDE OF ROCKPORT, THE Depression was taking its toll on the bottling business. Millions were out of work, and carbonated beverages, which had long been marketed as a luxury and an indulgence, were now being viewed as exactly that by families struggling even to put food on the table.

Soda fountains, bottlers and retailers were going belly-up by the thousands. Even those retailers that did manage to stay in business often found it difficult to afford to keep much stock on their shelves. A Coca-Cola executive noted in a 1932 memo: "There has been a tremendous loss in outlets. We have found that practically all bottlers are experiencing an inability on the part of many of their small outlets to buy more than one case and pay cash."

While Coca-Cola battled just to keep its sales steady, others could only dream of faring so well. Hires Root Beer, for example, watched its numbers plummet by 60 percent. Pepsi, since its bankruptcy in 1923, had passed through the hands of several owners and investors, and the Depression was not being kind to the current owner, the Loft Candy Company, either. The company even offered to sell to Coca-Cola at one point. Faced with its own issues, however, Coke executives declined to even make an offer.

Twin Lights, somehow, remained an anomaly. In fact, its numbers were fine, thanks in large part to the influx of tourists into Rockport in the summer.

Luckily for Twin Lights, this was a typically well-heeled clientele, for whom the Depression did not mean giving up luxuries (such as summer travel or carbonated beverages) entirely, if at all.

On top of that, Twin Lights had become something of a Christmas tradition for Cape Ann residents, providing a second perennial sales boost for the company, around the holidays. Pierce stated, "Ginger ale was the big seller used from mixers with whisky during the entire holiday season."

Lastly, any fears that the end of Prohibition (December 1933) would make a dent in the soft drink industry never made it up to Twin Lights' territory. A historically dry town even before Prohibition, Rockport did permit liquor sales for a few short years in the 1930s. But any impact on Twin Lights' sales was negligible.

Only a child at the time, Pierce still remembers the Depression era: "I know times were tough, but Twin Lights always seemed to flourish. Of course, then came the war. Things were even tougher then, but, still, we managed to get by OK. All things considered; business was good."

In fact, business was good enough that, in 1939, the company decided to make what would be the most significant purchase in its history. That year, it took delivery on a gleaming new automatic Dixie bottling machine for $2,500 that is still in use today. Production became faster and more efficient than ever.

Pierce loved to demonstrate how the machine worked. When I took his photo, he had a big smile on his face as he explained every movement of the machine as the bottles were filled with syrup and carbonated water then capped immediately and moved on to the round table, where each bottle was tipped upside down to make sure it was properly mixed, then placed in a wood case.

That year marked the beginning of World War II, however, with the United States becoming fully involved at the end of 1941. Suddenly, resources such as bottles were in short supply. One of the most significant considerations for soft drink bottlers became the rationing of sugar, a key ingredient. The Philippines, then a primary source for sugar, had been captured by the Japanese, reducing sugar imports to America by one-third. As a result, sugar was the first food item rationed in the United States, starting in the spring of 1942 and continuing until 1947. Most bottlers had their sugar supply cut in half.

"Our production was definitely limited because of the sugar rationing," remembers Pierce. As a result, the war also created a secondary market, for those so inclined. Pierce recalls one particularly memorable incident:

Pierce Sears stands in front of the Dixie bottling machine on the left. It was supplied by Crown Cork and Seal in 1939. *Author's collection.*

I can remember being very young, probably nine or 10, so this would have been early 40s, around 1943. A large car stopped outside our house, at the end of the driveway, and these two characters get out. I mean...I took one look at them and, even being as young as I was at the time, I knew they were not from around town, let us just say. I thought, "these guys look like gangsters." Gangsters were becoming prevalent at the time, and you would see in the newspaper about gangsters in Chicago and such. So, I could tell there was something going on with these guys. I was next door, in the house, and I watched them get out of the car, walk up the steps to the factory and go into the office where my grandfather was. A few minutes went by, and they came out again. They got back in the car and drove off, and I never saw them again. Years later, I learned that they were selling black market sugar, and they were trying to sell to my grandfather. He wasn't going to tie up with anything like that, so he said, "thanks, but no thanks," and sent them on their way.

But it was indicative of the climate at the time, and there were likely some businesses in the area that did bend to the secondary market. "It was a difficult time," says Pierce. "There were stores we delivered to during the war for whom even a nickel increase in the price of a case would have started a war of its own. Even trying to go up by a penny was significant at that time."

THERE WERE TWO FURTHER developments during this period that it would be remiss not to mention, as they would each have a notable impact on the industry going forward.

First, there was the debut in the mid-1930s of applied color labels (ACL) on bottles. This was the process by which labels with text and artwork could be effectively painted and baked onto the glass, eliminating the need for the repeated application of paper labels each time a bottle was refilled. This advance was something of a game-changer, as it was both timesaving and money-saving for bottlers (not to mention genuine objet d'art in the eyes of bottle collectors). Twin Lights' bottle supplier, Thatcher Glass of New York, developed its own proprietary version of the process, which they called "Pyroglazing." However, it would be a few more years before Joe or George Sears took the plunge into ACL bottles, choosing to stick with paper labels and signature bottle shapes until the end of the war. It is a strange coincidence that their bottle supplier was Thatcher Glass of New York (although it is not spelled like the island). Pierce still has the original proof paper copies from 1950 of the first ACL glass bottle designs for quarts and eight-ounce sizes.

Second, a visionary marketing move by Coca-Cola primed the brand for national, if not global, dominance after the war. Advertising had proved to be crucial for Coke in the 1920s, helping to establish the product as America's drink. But the Depression had wiped away a lot of that momentum in the

1930s, and Coke would need to rebound, just like everybody else. One of the ways the company did it is described here.

Coca-Cola executives and U.S. Army officials decided it would be a good morale booster to deliver bottles of Coke to the troops. The Coke execs vowed to ensure that, no matter where in the world they might be stationed, any person in uniform would be able to enjoy a Coke for five cents (the long-held retail price for a 6.5-ounce bottle of Coke). Initially, millions of bottles were shipped to the troops. But soon, actual makeshift bottling plants were set up as close to the front lines as was practical across Europe, North Africa and the South Pacific. The army "enlisted" more than one hundred Coca-Cola employees to oversee the operations (they were affectionately dubbed "Coca-Cola Colonels"). The execution was tricky (two Coke employees were killed in the line of duty), but the company ultimately managed to distribute some five billion Cokes to servicemen and servicewomen in even the most remote locations around the world.

The South Pacific proved a challenge, one that was ultimately solved by an Australian Coke bottler who offered the use of an old portable soda fountain for a base nearby. It proved such a perfect solution that the U.S. Army immediately requested another one hundred of them. The units became known as "jungle fountains," and more than one thousand were "deployed" in the Pacific theater. Despite the initial shipment getting torpedoed, the operation ensured that soldiers could enjoy "the pause that refreshes" even while at war.

The operation also afforded Coca-Cola a profound level of brand loyalty (not to mention brand recognition around the world). After the war, Coke surged in popularity like never before. But it was not the only thing surging. The soft drink industry was picking up again, and so was production. As soldiers returned home from the war seeking a new means of income, many were inspired to start up bottling businesses of their own. A second bottling bubble was underway.

Chapter 9

POSTWAR BOOM (1946–1949)

Following the war, the economy was stimulated again, and business was coming back strong for the soft drink industry. As soldiers returned home and sought a means of income, many were attracted to the bottling trade and set up shop. (It is not impossible to imagine that Coke's wartime bottling plants and jungle fountains had at least a little something to do with this.) Once again, it was a pivotal time for the industry—and for Twin Lights.

The immediate postwar years (1946–48) saw an unprecedented number of new bottlers go into business. It was the biggest bubble for soft drinks and bottling since the 1920s, with new brands and labels emerging every week. Ask any bottle collector, and they will tell you just how mind-boggling the level of activity was during this period. Christopher Weide, publisher of the directory series *Soft Drink Bottlers of the United States* (and Guinness World Record holder for the largest known collection of American soda bottles), has a unique perspective on the bottling industry. "It was *crazy*," he says, especially as many of these new bottlers seemed to be around for only a few years. "Because by the late 1940s, and certainly by the time you get into the 1950s, many of these names had already come and gone."

In 1946, business at Twin Lights was as good as ever. "After the war, we were back to leaving ten to twelve cases at a time at stores around Christmastime," says Pierce. "Producing five hundred cases a day was a good day at the

The work gang in 1944, from left to right: Pierce's grandfather Joe Sears, Beefo Johnson, Bill "Ole" Oleson, Chuck Rowe and George Sears (Pierce's father). *Pierce Sears collection.*

factory." There was a big, new truck in the yard, and Joe Sears, having weathered both the Depression and the war, was feeling bullish.

The work gang in 1944 consisted of Pierce's grandfather Joe Sears, Beefo Johnson, Bill "Ole" Oleson, Chuck Rowe and George Sears (father of Pierce).

The last of the three Blatchford Brothers, Gilman Blatchford, had handed control of the Gloucester-based company to his son William toward the end of the 1920s. William ran the company throughout the Depression and the war. But by the time the war ended, he was ready to exit the business, and, in 1946, Joe Sears struck a deal with William to buy him out. And so it was that Twin Lights made its sole acquisition, of Blatchford Brothers bottling works of Gloucester.

Joe Sears did not want to stop there. A sizable industrial space at 431 East Main Street in Gloucester (which today houses Steve Connolly Seafood) had become available, and Joe had his eye on it. His dream of expansion could become a reality in this larger space, affording Twin Lights increased production capacity.

"My grandfather would have loved to expand. He really wanted to move the business up there into that space," explain Pierce. "But I'm not sure whether my father was as keen on the idea."

If father and son had diverging visions for the business, it was reflective of their two personalities. Joe Sears was an entrepreneur who had built up the business from nothing. He had spent forty years growing the company and was entrepreneurially inclined to continue that growth. George Sears recognized that any expansion at this stage would mean a change in the structure of the operation. He enjoyed running the company and being in charge. He also enjoyed his community involvement, volunteering for Rockport Fire and Rescue, as his father had done, for example. He drove the ladder truck for twenty-nine years and the ambulance for thirty-four years. He had a weakness for Cadillacs (see the town ambulance, a white Cadillac, in the accompanying image). Pierce also drove Cadillacs for a few years when his father willed him the Cadillac Brougham after his death. Today, he is driving a fire-engine-red Buick. George loved the fact that he could stay active with both the volunteer fire department and the Rockport ambulance service. He was connected by radio from his office to both groups, which were stationed close by just a block down Broadway. Keeping the business at a manageable level meant that, not only could he avoid ceding any aspects of control over the business (which he felt was running just fine as it was, thank you), but also that he would be certain to still have time for auxiliary activities. George Sears, in so many words, was

George Sears, who drove the Rockport Town ambulance for thirty-seven years, poses in front of the new one in 1962. *Pierce Sears collection.*

perfectly happy with his current quality of life and saw no reason to upset the root beer cart.

In 1949, the debate became moot. Twin Lights would lose its second (and last surviving) founder when Joe Sears died in the spring of that year. His grandson Pierce remembers him fondly. "Joe Sears was a real gentleman. A serious fella, but a very generous man," he recalls. "He lived here on the premises, so he was always the first one in the office in the morning. In the evening he loved to smoke a pipe. He had a whole stack of them. He would sit in his rocking chair with a pipe, listening to Lowell Thomas or Jimmie Fidler on the radio and catch up on the day's newspapers. He was a kind man, and well liked."

Pierce Sears would have his own minor brush with death that year, in the autumn. A senior at Rockport High School, Pierce was seventeen and took the company pickup truck (a 1946 Chevy) out one Friday night. The Rockport High graduating class that year had ten boys in it. "And I had half of them in the truck," says Pierce. Following a night of bowling in

Gloucester, the group decided to drive down to Beverly to get some food at a place called the Chicken Coop. With Pierce was George Korpi, Martin Mansfield, John Korpi, Richard Balzarini and Charles Johnson. Afterward, with three in the truck's cab and three in back sitting in the bed of the truck, they set out for home, rambling back up Route 127 in Manchester. A 1940 Mercury driven by Irene Ryan of Beverly Farms traveling in the opposite direction swerved suddenly into their lane and hit the truck head-on. The three boys in the back were sent flying into the road, while the three in front sat stunned. Word of the accident came into the Rockport Police Department, and an officer sped to the scene with George Sears in tow. Mrs. Ryan suffered a fractured left arm and minor lacerations. In the final tally, Pierce was the only one to come out of it with any serious injuries (a broken kneecap that was wired back together at Addison Gilbert Hospital in Gloucester a couple of weeks later). Nobody was more relieved than Pierce's father, George. If there was any silver lining to be found, it was that at least he could now buy another new truck.

The accident scene in Manchester. The 1940 Mercury looks the worse for wear compared to the heavy Twin Lights pickup truck. *Pierce Sears collection.*

Pierce and his father, George, pictured in front of the "Big Blue Truck" in 1990.
Pierce Sears collection.

A brand-new 1949 blue Ford truck was added to the fleet, and as had become customary, a local painter named Everett Ranta was summoned to hand-paint the company name on the side. The format had been updated as follows:

Thomas Wilson & Co
Twin Lights Beverages
Ginger Ale
Rockport

Chapter 10

HAPPY DAYS (1950–1960)

My earliest memories of buying Twin Lights Tonic is about seven years old," recalls Rockport native Chester Clark, who grew up on School Street across from what is now the Rockport Public Library (then the Tarr School) in the 1940s and '50s. "My mother had started giving me an allowance of twenty-five cents a week (and my grandmother would sometimes supplement that). I would go across the street to Broadway Garage, where they kept a cooler full of tonic to tempt thirsty motorists. Its location was where the Rockport Market is today. If they didn't have the flavor I wanted that day—there were so many flavors back then—I could walk up the street to the next place. Twin Lights Tonic really was ubiquitous. They sold it at team games, they sold it at the yacht club, we sold it at high school dances, and they would sell it with lobsters on Bearskin Neck."

Twin Lights, like the rest of the soft drink industry and like America itself, was enjoying a period of considerable prosperity in the 1950s. The economy grew by some 37 percent during the decade. Summertime at the Twin Lights factory would see almost a dozen employees washing, bottling and delivering. Twin Lights was everywhere on Cape Ann. Says Pierce, "We really did have just about every store, every bar, every tavern, every restaurant."

By the time he was a teenager, Chester Clark had a job working down the street from Twin Lights. "My friends, Bill Parsons and Charlie Cleaves, both worked there at 'the tonic factory', as we used to call it," he remembers. "I used to head up there after I got out of work and wait for them to get out.

But sometimes they ended up doing long days—during peak season, there were twelve-hour days sometimes."

Summer had always been peak "tonic season," but postwar and into the 1950s, the business started to change. Pierce explains:

> *Traditionally, we always had a big slow-down after Labor Day. Once fall arrived, you would have this ritual of taking in a lot of empties from places that closed for the winter. There was a big section of the garage where we brought in hundreds of cases. We are talking two hundred to three hundred cases. You would dump them all out and they would need to be sorted— separate the large and small bottles, the greens from the whites, and such. Then we would clean all the bottles and put them away for the winter. In the spring we would take them all back out, wash them again, and fill them back up. It was that much of a difference between summer and the rest of the year back then. But after the war, gradually, winter picked up. It got busier and busier until, eventually, there was no longer any yearly "put-away" of the bottles, it just became year-round.*

Pierce estimates that Twin Lights was delivering to around two hundred accounts by this time. It was busy. They had a big truck and a little truck, Pierce explains. The big truck went to Gloucester. The little truck was used around Rockport. On an average day, they would start loading the trucks at 8:00 a.m. and be on the road by 9:00 a.m.

"Danny would always be on the big truck," says Pierce. Danny was Danny Stanwood, a nephew of Joe Sears who, for years, drove the two-ton stake bed truck. Danny served in the U.S. Navy during World War II and went to work for Twin Lights upon his return. "My memory of Danny is of a trim, dapper fellow who always had perfectly combed hair," says Chester Clark. "He must have carried thousands of cases of tonic in and out of restaurants, stores, bars and homes during his time there."

Danny worked for Twin Lights into the 1980s before retiring to Florida, where he died in 1994. But he was the main man on deliveries for a long time, according to Pierce. "He would be out all day, probably stop to eat lunch at one of the delivery stops, and then usually get back around 3:30–4:00 p.m. Depending on how early or late he got back, we'd either unload the empties that afternoon or leave them until morning. The majority of stops would just pay upon delivery, so Danny would come in with a wad of cash and all the invoice slips in a book he carried with him, hand them to my dad, and it would all go in the safe."

The Monday route, for example, would be into downtown Gloucester, "all through Main Street, down to the fort," explains Pierce. The "fort" area of Gloucester is one of the oldest sections, dating to 1743. It is known as the old fort on Commercial Street and now includes several private homes, fish sheds and fish processing plants. Cape Pond Ice Company was completed in 1949. On this point, selected strategically, is a hill that effectively commands the inner harbor. Breastworks were thrown up, and eight twelve-pounders were placed in position in the fort. The reason for the fort was the fear of French incursions, which were never realized. As early as 1703, efforts were made to fortify the area. Today, it is home to a new luxury hotel called Beauport, which would have been a profitable customer for Twin Lights Beverages.

Wednesday was East Gloucester: "There were so many small stops that it was time-consuming. Little restaurants, small and medium grocery stores, vending machines." Tuesdays and Thursday were usually spent in the factory, and then Friday might be another swing around the Cape and a swoop down into Essex.

Pierce usually drove the smaller truck and handled the Rockport deliveries. For years, when he was younger, he rode with his father on the Rockport routes and with Danny on the Gloucester routes. He and Danny both knew all the routes by memory and sometimes even swapped with each other for a change of scenery.

Ask Pierce to take you through an average day on deliveries, and he still remembers just about all the stops. He had hit many of the hotels and inns: the Turk's Head Inn, Ocean View, the Seaward Inn down by the U.S. Coast Guard station. There was the Emerson Inn (named for Ralph Waldo Emerson, who had stayed there), where deliveries were made to the kitchen and the beverage was served to guests in the dining room, and a second inn owned by the same family on Granite Street, where he would need to stock the vending machine. The golf club, the American Legion Hall Post 98 and Rockport High School also had vending machines that required stocking. Vending machines had replaced wood ice chests, and whenever anyone requested a new machine, George Sears would order it for them from the Ideal company in Indiana.

Then there was MacDonald's (an eight-seat lunch counter and candy shop across from the train station), Roffey's (a small grocer and candy shop), Alfonse Thibault's hotdog and hamburger shack and Ranta's Market (another small family grocer). There was also Walima Market on Forrest Street, where they always remembered Pierce playing with their meat grinder when he was a kid on deliveries with his father. The staff would jokingly ask him if he still wanted to play with it when he made their deliveries as an adult.

Seaview Farm on South Street (Lane's Farm) had a roadside vegetable stand across the street that sold bottles of Twin Lights. Just recently, they reopened the farm stand. Although they no longer sell Twin Lights Tonic, they do sell beer and wine. In fact, roadside stands had become a significant new market for soft drink sales during this period, as more and more people across the country took to the road in their new cars.

Then it was on to Bearskin Neck, home to the famous Motif Number 1 and to numerous restaurants and other businesses that stocked Twin Lights. There were stops at the boat filling station on Tuna Wharf, followed by a private delivery for the Swiss owners of a haberdashery on the Neck that hosted many foreign guests in the summer. In fact, private home deliveries were as numerous as the commercial orders now. It was essential to keep bottles of Twin Lights on hand in the summer, and George Sears was happy to send his delivery team to homes.

Front Beach in those days was serviced by a now-legendary spot called Jimmy's Sunrise, a hotdog and ice cream stand where eating one of owner George "Jimmy" Rantilla's steamed dogs with a cold bottle of Twin Lights on the beach made for nothing short of a quintessential Rockport experience. The bottles were kept cold in a large ice cooler on the wood porch out front. "Getting tonic from a cooler in those days was a much different experience to how it's served today," says Chester Clark, a Jimmy's regular. "You'd open the cover and the bottles were usually arranged by flavor. They were stood in a few inches of water kept cold by a couple of blocks of ice, which was delivered daily, and you'd identify the flavors from looking at the caps."

Jimmy's was a favorite lunch stop for Pierce Sears, as well. The cooler on the porch, despite being filled mostly with bottles of Twin Lights, had a big Coca-Cola logo on its side. Since he was using their cooler, Jimmy must have felt it was only fair that he take a case of Coke now and then from the Coke delivery guy, so there were usually a few bottles of America's more famous cola in the cooler. Pierce insists that Coke tasted different back then—"much better," he says. How does he know? "Well, I used to grab a bottle of Coke for myself sometimes when I stopped to see Jimmy," he admits with a smile. "I think my dad certainly would have frowned on that if he knew." Pierce recalled that on a long Labor Day weekend (Saturday, Sunday and Monday), Jimmy's sold 120 cases of six-ounce bottles at Front

Front Beach was a hotbed of tourists and Twin Lights Tonic sales at Jimmy's Sunrise. *Author's collection.*

Beach (2,880 bottles). Pierce had to go back and forth many times to the factory to pick up more cases and return the empties. George Rantilla and Pierce were close friends and often opened the restaurant together on busy summer mornings.

Today, the same building houses Nate's Restaurant and still offers a takeout window for beachgoers across the street on Front Beach.

Twin Lights made a cola itself, but, with so many other flavors, it was never one of its biggest sellers. "The one place we did sell a lot of cola, because they used them for mixers, was in the saloons of Gloucester," says Pierce. "And there were a *lot* of them. There were a ton of places in Gloucester to go drink and that was a godsend for us. They did not have dispenser guns for their mixers then, so they would buy quart bottles from us—soda water, cola, Tom Collins and half-and-half. That was a big part of our business, and probably the biggest part of our cola business."

Elsewhere in Gloucester, Danny was delivering Twin Lights to businesses such as the office of the *Gloucester Times*, which had a vending machine. Because the paper's owner also owned with the *Beverly Times*, Danny was soon making the drive down Route 128 to deliver to their offices, too. Addison Gilbert Hospital in Gloucester used to take cases of Twin Lights Ginger Ale. "Our local doctor got us in there," Pierce reveals. "There were three doctors in Rockport at the time, and Dr. Green, who lived down the street from the factory, got us into the hospital in the early '60s. They used it for settling stomachs, giving to people with colds, things like that, and that lasted for thirty years, into the 1990s."

Oil painting of Jimmy's Sunrise Restaurant across from Front Beach by artist Wayne Morrell, circa 1962. *Author's collection.*

Nate's Restaurant is in the same building that once housed Jimmy's Sunrise. *Author's collection.*

Another driver for Twin Lights was Matteo "Tony" Maccarone, who had joined the team after retiring as a delivery driver for Pepsi in 1954. Tony would have a hand in expanding Twin Lights distribution beyond Gloucester and Rockport, into neighboring towns like Hamilton and Essex. These latter towns had been on his route for Pepsi, so he was able to open a lot of new accounts for Twin Lights, as he already knew them. He worked until 1980, moved to Florida and died in 1999 at the age of ninety. His friends all called him "Tony Macaroni."

This story was attested to and recounted by Pierce Sears himself as well as a local resident who once worked for Pierce, Eddie Everett, whom I interviewed for this book. An example of Tony's former Pepsi route connections was a now-defunct ski area in Hamilton called Hamilton Slopes, later Hamilton Ski-Tow. It was little more than a large hill with a tow-rope, but in the 1950s and '60s, there were dozens of such places around Massachusetts (before most were put out of business by property developers, rising liability costs and easier access to larger mountains up north via wide new highways). There was a makeshift lodge at the base of Hamilton Slopes where lift tickets were sold and a little snack bar was operated. Says Pierce: "That was a big bonus for us because winter was traditionally slow. We used to take sixty cases at a time up there in the '50s and '60s."

Then there were the even less traditional deliveries. "We delivered to fire stations, post offices, places like that," says Pierce. It was common back then for employees at these otherwise "official" buildings to have a side business selling snacks, gum and tonic. The local fire station, for example, kept a big cooler stocked, and if you were walking past, you could stop and buy a cold bottle for a quarter, or a pack of gum.

"The firefighters and postal workers used to order cases to keep in stock for themselves, basically, but they would also sell them on the side. That all ceased eventually as their superiors stepped in and government regulations put an end to it," says Pierce. "Those were different times."

Another side business for Twin Lights was the delivery of CO_2 tanks. There were a handful of soda fountains (and what used to be called "ice cream saloons") that, while they didn't sell bottles, would still get their "tubes" from George Sears for their fountains. These were places like the Ice Cream Junction in Hamilton and, closer to home, Poole's Rexall drugstore and Tuck's Candy, both of which used to have soda counters.

There was a familiar face working behind the soda counter at Tuck's in the 1950s, too: George's daughter, Cathie. Pierce's only sibling, Cathie Sears

Pierce's sister Cathie lived on Ten Pound Island as keeper with her U.S. Coast Guardsman husband in the early 1940s and later at Eastern Point Light. *Author's collection.*

did not end up working at Twin Lights, but lighthouses would continue to loom large in her life.

Cathie married a Coast Guardsman and lighthouse keeper whose first assignment after they wed was the Ten Pound Island Light located in Gloucester Harbor. (It was famously painted by Winslow Homer, among others, and he even lived with the keeper there for several years.) They lived on the tiny island for three years until the light was decommissioned. Next, they got stationed a couple of miles down the coast, becoming the keepers of Eastern Point Lighthouse (which Winslow Homer also painted). Cathie would go on to enjoy a successful professional career in California, where she and her husband still live today.

ALL IN ALL, THESE were happy days for Twin Lights Tonic. George Sears was enjoying his life, and he loved running the business. "We had a lot of good times," says Pierce. "But my father was not the kind of guy to take a lot of time off—he liked to work, and he spent a lot of late hours in the office. He would be out there into the night, because he did so much all

116

day and then had to spend the nighttime doing the books. Plus, he had the community stuff he did with the ambulance service and such. My mother would worry about him. I remember back during the big hurricane in 1938, my mother was alone in the house up at 1 Granite Street with the roof leaking worrying sick about him because he was out running around town helping people."

But George would reward himself with a new Cadillac every few years, and he enjoyed the occasional road trip. Family vacations were relatively modest affairs, often driving trips that might include stops to visit other bottlers or to attend the annual Boston & Gloucester Convention in Atlantic City.

"My father was constantly roaming around," says Pierce. "Even if we were on a vacation or something, he would stop in to visit other bottlers— whether he knew them yet or not. He was very curious about how others were running their operations, and he would stop in, make friends and often ended up having lasting relationships with many of these other owners. I suspect he was also probably picking up a few helpful tips here and there and using whatever he was learning from these visits when he got back home."

The annual bottler's conventions were always a source of amusement for Pierce. "They'd alternate years, small and big, so every other year was a really big one, where they had all the machines on display. We went to the big ones. All the major companies, like Coke and Pepsi, had booths and big displays. The manufacturers all had their newest and biggest equipment. Then you would have companies like Squirt Soda there with a little person dressed up as 'Li'l Squirt' to promote their brand, or another brand would have a magician doing tricks. It was a different time in the '60s," he laughs. "So, these things were considered to be entertaining."

In 1959, the building that houses the Twin Lights factory underwent a major remodeling. The big, forty-foot "Thomas Wilson & Co" sign was taken down by the painters and ended up being left in the back of the garage indefinitely instead of going back on the building. A second new bottle-washing machine had been purchased in 1953, and another new one followed in 1965. This newest one is the machine still in use today. Made by the Ladewig Company, it's a surprisingly beautiful piece of American craftsmanship that was proudly presented to George Sears, like all of Ladewig's machines at the time, with a large cast aluminum plaque affixed to the side of it:

The Ladewig bottle washer, purchased in 1965, continues in use today. It can take six rows of bottles, which are washed and rinsed twice. *Pierce Sears collection.*

Pierce proudly operates the bottle washer. *Pierce Sears collection.*

LADEWIG BOTTLE WASHER
Built Expressly For
THOMAS WILSON & COMPANY
ROCKPORT, MASSACHUSETTS
Archie Ladewig Co. Waukesha, Wis. U.S.A.

"That arrived at Christmas time in 1965, it was brand new," remembers Pierce. "It was up and running in January 1966, and still running today. We got a six-wide, to take six bottles at a time, but they also made them bigger: eight-wide, twelve-wide, twenty-four-wide. It was the primo washer of its day." This is a gigantic thirty-foot-long machine that washes and rinses the bottles twice.

For a small, independent bottler on Cape Ann, everything was business as usual. Elsewhere around the country, however, the industry was undergoing a paradigm shift that would change the carbonated soft drink industry for good.

Chapter 11

CONSOLIDATION (1960–1990)

The 1950s and 1960s were a boom time for Twin Lights. Up here on Cape Ann, it remained blissfully immune to the commercial changes going on around it. In the rest of the country, however, a period of historic change was underway for the bottling industry with the start of consolidation. The changes would be drastic, lasting and swift, taking place with a momentum not seen since the initial bottling boom of the early 1900s, when Twin Lights began. By the time all was said and done, the soft drink industry would be controlled by just five major companies. Small independent bottlers like Twin Lights would be an anomaly.

During the massive postwar bubble, the number of bottling plants in the United States peaked at an estimated 6,700 in the early 1950s. From this point on, that number would decrease—rapidly and permanently. Regional footprints were growing as small neighboring bottlers merged operations. Often, these were bottlers for the same brand (e.g., Pepsi), but it was also happening with bottlers of competing brands—for example, mergers between 7UP and Royal Crown bottlers.

Simultaneously, consumption was on the rise, and the overall cost of doing business for bottlers was declining. As time went on, packaging and distribution became cheaper as bottlers shifted to nonreturnable cans and then plastic. In addition, advancements in trucking (including elements as simple as better roads) and the growth of supermarket chains (coinciding with the erosion of smaller mom-and-pop grocers) made distribution more efficient. All of this favored economy of scale. Bigger was better—and more profitable.

Christopher Weide, the renowned collector and author, points directly to the late 1950s as the starting point for this trend. "The so-called Big Five—Coke, Pepsi, 7UP, Dr Pepper and RC Cola—ultimately forced the mom-and-pop bottlers out of business," he says. "By the late 1950s to early 1960s, there were very few independent bottlers left."

In 1960, the four largest companies (Coke, Pepsi, RC Cola and 7UP) accounted for 72 to 75 percent of total soft drink sales, with Coca-Cola grabbing about 37 percent of that. (In 1962, Dr Pepper, previously a regional brand, went national, establishing the Big Five.)

This takeover of the marketplace was accomplished by a few different means.

"In order to get their product in the store, Coke and Pepsi went to supermarket chains and offered to 'lease' shelf space, which they would come in and stock every month," explains Weide. "The little guys couldn't compete with that."

In some cases, this even involved exclusivity agreements that went so far as to restrict the shelves to "national brands only" to remove local product. Notably, none of these brands dared go so far as to try to edge out their big (national) competitors, though.

For most local bottlers, this meant they were becoming limited to local corner grocery stores or selling from the plant. Luckily for Twin Lights, this had always been the business model, and as a result, it continued to thrive well into the 1980s. "That was our savior back in those days, that there were so many mom-and-pop stores," acknowledges Pierce. "There were two chain supermarkets in Rockport back then, First National and A&P, but we never stocked our tonic in there. We were a small-scale business."

Pierce also adds: "From the '70s on, too, you had malls come in, big-box stores, giant supermarkets....More and more, that's where people would shop. We could not do now what we did back then, going up against that kind of competition. We were never geared toward supermarkets."

The expansion of grocery store chains was another factor that hastened consolidation and pushed neighboring regional bottlers to merge with one another. At the time, a single large grocery chain, spread over multiple states, might find itself negotiating with multiple individual bottlers of the same brand, in different territories, each with a potentially different price offer, to boot. Any buyer for a large chain preferred to place one order, with one vendor, for one set price.

In other instances, one of the Big Five might come in and offer to buy out an independent bottler with an offer that was simply too good to refuse—in some cases, ten times what they might earn in a typical year, which made selling out a no-brainer. Says Weide, "For most of these guys, they would make more selling their business to Coke than they could make over the rest of the lifetime of their business." After buying the operation, in many cases, the large brands would then simply shut them down.

The 1970s also signaled the end for soda fountains and ice cream parlors, which swiftly declined with the emergence of fast-food restaurants, vending machines and commercial/soft-serve ice cream. "Once places started switching to premixes," says Pierce, "my father decided not to get into that, so we lost some of that business in the '60s and '70s. But we did still provide the [CO_2] tanks for a few places."

BY 1980, THE BIG Five accounted for about 80 percent of total soft drink sales. Notably, a whopping 75 percent of these sales were now colas. Chelmsford, a major brand in the 1950s and '60s, had plummeted to just 2 percent market share by the mid-'70s. Consumer preference had changed considerably.

The 1980s brought even further consolidation, as Coke and Pepsi began acquiring many of their own bottlers. Previously, these plants were under contract only to purchase the syrups and bottle the product. But now, in this wave of consolidation, they were being brought under the same corporate umbrella. In some cases, Coke and Pepsi bottlers were even taking over 7UP and Dr Pepper franchises.

By 1990, the number of bottling plants in the United States was down to about eight hundred. By 2000, that number had shrunk even smaller, to just five hundred—this from a high of more than ten times that number only fifty years prior.

There were few surviving independent operations by this time. Twin Lights was one of them. At the other end of the spectrum was another Massachusetts company, Polar Beverages. Polar's determination to stay competitive had led to it becoming a "super regional" beverage company, having completed some thirty acquisitions and franchise bottling such brands as Adirondack, A&W, Seagram, 7UP, Royal Crown, Snapple, Fiji Water and Nantucket Nectars. It also formed a joint venture with the Cott Corporation (another memorable name for New England soda drinkers of a certain age). The largest independent beverage company in the United States, Polar Beverages is a purveyor of premium-quality sparkling beverages, including Polar® Seltzer, heritage sodas and Polar Orange Dry. It was founded in Worcester, Massachusetts, in 1882 by a savvy bartender, Denis Crowley, who recognized opportunity in carbonation as Prohibition began to rumble in New England. He crafted what he considered the best-tasting bubble recipe and began selling sparkling beverages from a horse-drawn carriage. Today, the company remains owned and operated by the family's fourth and fifth generations.

Keurig Dr Pepper (KDP) and Polar Beverages jointly announced on July 30, 2020, that they had entered into a long-term franchise agreement that will provide national distribution to Polar Seltzer sparkling seltzer waters.

Family-owned and operated since 1882, Polar Seltzer is the third-largest branded flavored sparkling water (according to a press release issued by both KDP and Polar) in the United States, despite availability in less than 35 percent of the country. Where distributed, it is the fastest turning sparkling water. Polar Seltzer brands come in more than thirty-five varieties.

Longtime partners, Polar Beverages has manufactured and distributed key KDP brands in its Northeast territories for over three decades. With this new agreement, KDP expands the partnership by now manufacturing, distributing and selling Polar Seltzer in much of its direct store delivery footprint. Polar will continue to manufacture and distribute its sparkling water in its existing territories, as will select Polar distributors.

Polar was also now supplementing its business by making private-label and "store brand" soft drinks. One notable development from this is the rebirth of Chelmsford Golden Ginger Ale. Founded in 1901 as the Chelmsford Spring Company, the company sold its ginger beer in stone bottles before eventually changing to glass (and changing its name to Chelmsford Ginger Ale Company). Soon, it was distributing throughout New England and, at one point, even rivaling Coca-Cola in popularity. Canada Dry bought it in 1931 as part of a major expansion effort and continued to produce Chelmsford's unique ginger ale, even following subsequent acquisitions by Dr Pepper and then Schweppes in the 1980s. But production ceased in 2003, much to the dismay of locals. Shortly thereafter, the New England supermarket chain Market Basket (aka DeMoula's) approached Polar (which was already producing its other store-brand sodas) to ask about making a Chelmsford Golden Ginger Ale for them. According to a 2014 article in *Boston Magazine*, Polar was never able to acquire the original formula, but it managed to reverse-engineer an approximation of the original, close enough to keep the die-hard loyalists happy.

Today, the Big Five is down to a Big Three, with Coke and Pepsi controlling close to 75 percent of market share. In 1997 (the year I retired from A&W Brands), as part of the ownership group that the year, we sold the company to Cadbury Schweppes. Dr Pepper, 7UP and RC Cola eventually merged under the umbrella of Cadbury Schweppes, which then became Dr Pepper Snapple Group. This group now had in its stable all the Schweppes brands, A&W Root Beer and Cream Soda, Sunkist, Vernor's, Canada Dry products, Barrelhead Root Beer, Squirt, Hires, 7UP, RC, Nehi, Crush, IBC Root Beer, Sun Drop, Orangina, Hawaiian Punch and Yoo Hoo, along with all the Snapple products of juices, teas and energy drinks. In 2018, the entire company was acquired by Keurig Green Mountain Inc. Coffee Company.

Keurig Dr Pepper (KDP) is a leading beverage company in North America, with annual revenue of more than $11 billion and nearly 26,000 employees. KDP holds leadership positions in soft drinks, specialty coffee and tea, water, juice and juice drinks and mixers, and it markets the number-one single-serve coffee brewing system in the United States and Canada. The company's portfolio of more than 125 owned, licensed and partner brands is designed to satisfy virtually any consumer need, any time.

Interestingly, in 2017, Coca-Cola undertook a "re-franchising" effort to divest from nearly seventy of its bottling plants and return them to local, independent ownership.

Massachusetts has been home to a plethora of beloved soft drink brands through the years. In the 1950s, Boston Red Sox legend Ted Williams was drinking Moxie before he started to drink his own Ted's Root Beer, and Clicquot Club was one of the largest soft drink companies in America. But today, only a tiny handful of the early independent bottlers remain across the Northeast. They meet up once a year as members of a group called the New England Independent Bottlers Association (NEIBA) to discuss industry updates and even strategize on group purchases. Among them is Squamscot Beverages (founded in 1863) in New Hampshire; Yacht Club (1915) and Empire Bottling Works (1930), both in Rhode Island; Avery's Beverages (1904), Foxon Park (1922) and Hosmer Mountain Spring (1912), all in Connecticut; and Simpson Spring (1878) in Easton, Massachusetts. Then, of course, there is Twin Lights (1907) in Rockport. For the time being, at least.

Chapter 12

THE LAST KEEPER

In decades past, customers would call the Twin Lights office and, if George Sears was not there to answer the phone, they would leave their order on the answering machine. Nowadays, when you phone Pierce at home, the message is pretty much the same: "Leave your order, or your message, at the tone."

In 1993, George Sears, the man who guided Twin Lights through the previous fifty years and its most prosperous period, passed away at the age of eighty-eight. Like his father, Joe Sears, he worked right up until the day he died. He had already taught Pierce everything there was to know about running the company—even if he was reluctant to take his hands off the wheel and let someone else drive—and he had written everything out, anyway, just in case.

Today, carbonated soft drinks are a roughly $48 billion industry with 90 percent market penetration. For Twin Lights, however, business is gradually winding down. In fact, Pierce distributes Twin Lights now only via private home deliveries. "It's really just a hobby now, not a business," he says. "It effectively stopped being a business three to four years ago once we got out of the retail side."

The compressor on the refrigeration unit broke a few years ago. Rather than replace it, Pierce just makes sure to bottle when it is cold outside. Colder water absorbs the CO_2 better and makes for better carbonation, he always says. "So, we must pick our days now when we plan to bottle. It's usually only in the winter these days."

Frankly, this is fine with Pierce Sears. After all, he is eighty-eight now and he has been running the company pretty much by himself for the last twenty-five years and working there since 1956, a total of sixty-four years. The current amount of business is just enough to fire up the machines a couple of times a year and then go visit the loyal customers whom he has known, in most cases, for decades. "As long as it doesn't lose money and the customers still want it," he says, "I'll keep doing it." Plus, it means he can still donate a few cases here and there to community causes, charity events, the Little League and things like that, carrying on the community-minded tradition that's been a part of Twin Lights' DNA since the start.

It takes three people to do a bottling run: one to load the Ladewig washer, where a pulley transports the bottles and then feeds the washed bottles into the Dixie ("the filler"); a second person to man the Dixie, basically keeping an eye out in case a bottle falls over on its way out of the washer or something; and then a third person to do the labeling and a quick upside-down turn of the bottle to mix the ingredients as it comes out of the Dixie before placing it in the crate. Today, with their small runs, Pierce usually manages the latter two tasks himself, requiring just two people in total.

The Dixie remains, aside from Pierce, the heart and soul of the plant. In fact, the two are only a few years apart in age. Pierce says it is a miracle that Dixie still runs, and that is all down to an anonymous friend of his who first worked at Twin Lights starting in 1960 as a teenager. The young man was always curious about the machinery and, luckily, George Sears was happy to indulge him. The fellow would go on to become a full-time machinist but returned in the late 1980s, as George's health was declining, to help out with the Dixie and Ladewig machines. "If it wasn't for him," Pierce says flatly, "I wouldn't have been able to keep that machine going on my own. I am not mechanically inclined and this machine…it is ancient, it is balky. But this guy can break down Dixie into all its bits and pieces, figure out what is wrong, and put it all back together again within two to three hours—with no parts left over!"

For now, there are several dozen wooden cases with full bottles of Twin Lights tonic stacked up against the wall inside the factory: birch beer, lemon-lime, root beer, strawberry, plain soda and the signature ginger ale, as well as a couple of cases of diet ginger ale that Pierce makes especially for one particular longtime customer.

The only brand Twin Lights ever made outside of its own was Moxie. George Sears had picked up the Moxie franchise for the area after the war, and die-hard fans of the product used to drive from miles around to pick it

Old wood cases still stacked in the Twin Lights Beverages factory. *Pierce Sears collection.*

up at the factory in Rockport when it became harder to find in later years. "We used to drive down to Boston to pick up the Moxie syrup at the factory," remembers Pierce. "It was a beautiful stone and brick building, clean as a whistle and had a Moxie fountain."

In 1966, Moxie was sold to a company in Atlanta, and after that, the syrup was shipped up from Georgia. In 2010, a New England company owned by Coca-Cola bought the rights to Moxie, and Pierce received a "cease and desist" letter in the mail. "I got this nasty letter out of nowhere threatening to sue," says Pierce, shaking his head. "Heck, I live up here at the ends of the earth, I had no idea the company was sold. We had been bottling Moxie forever. I called them up and they were nice about it in the end. But I still had some syrup left, so I just used that up. It lasted a few more months, and that was the last Moxie I sold."

Meanwhile, bottles had become a major problem for the business over the last two decades—mainly, that they just were not coming back from the stores. These are not any old bottles. They are thick, glass returnables. While bottles today might have a deposit on them, they are not washed and refilled—they are made of a cheaper, thinner glass that is crushed and recycled. Pierce's older machines cannot use those bottles because they are too brittle. The bottles he can use are not available anymore, unless they can be found on the secondary market.

Pierce did just that for the first several years, buying up literal truckloads of old bottles from defunct bottlers or from bottlers that were converting to nonreturnable bottles and getting rid of their old refillable ones. He went all around Massachusetts, New Hampshire, wherever he could find them. "I bought, literally, thousands of cases of old bottles," he says. "One time, I had a tractor trailer come in from Pennsylvania with three hundred to four hundred cases on it."

One interesting bottle was by Lake View Beverages from Webster, Massachusetts. On the back of the bottle is imprinted "Bottled Near Lake Chargoggagoggmanchauggagoggchaubunagungamaugg." This lake, also known as Webster Lake, is about 1,400 acres in area. It was named by a local newspaperman in 1921. The name is forty-five letters and fourteen syllables long. It is the longest name of any geographic feature in all the United States. It has been translated as "fishing place at the boundary" by anthropologist Ives Goddard. A more humorous translation is, "You fish on your side, I'll fish on my side, and no one shall fish in the middle."

But Pierce could not keep up with the loss of the bottles at retail, no matter how many times he raised the deposit on them. He was losing them, he says, at a rate of 70 to 80 percent. Then collectability became a problem. A Twin Lights bottle these days can fetch twenty dollars on eBay, far more than the twenty-cent deposit. It is the same with many vintage bottles now, which makes it nearly impossible to find them on the secondary market in any kind of bulk.

THE CONSUMER SOFT DRINK market, despite its sizable numbers, has experienced more than ten consecutive years of decline. There is a certain irony in the fact that what began as a health drink and a "tonic" would, a century later, become demonized for being something quite the opposite. But public and legislative debate targeting sugary drinks as a key cause of obesity (a documented health crisis in the United States today) is one reason. The Twin Lights vending machine at Rockport High School, it is worth noting, was taken out a long time ago.

At the same time, consumers have been pivoting toward more health-conscious products in general. The concern about soft drinks is not new. It can be traced back as far as the 1940s. But that concern has only continued to grow, because, well, so did consumption. Average annual soft drink consumption in 1950 was 10.8 gallons per person. In 2000, that number was 49.3 gallons.

Big soda brands have taken some measures in response to this. These include packaging in smaller serving sizes, using low-calorie and natural sweeteners and, strategically, adding more products like iced tea, kombucha, fruit beverages, coconut water and, of all things, bottled natural spring water. In at least one respect, the industry has come full circle.

It is not all bad news, however. Retro brands and "craft sodas" have enjoyed a small resurgence in recent years. In step with the larger trend among millennials toward vintage and "authentic" brands, as well as products they deem to be more wholesome or "real," some older soft drink labels have been revived in much the same way that dormant clothing labels and beer brands have been recently, providing an uptick in business for some independent bottlers.

Orca Beverages, a company in Washington State, has made a business out of producing and distributing a variety of regional and old-time soda brands such as Dad's Root Beer, Spiffy Cola, Jic Jac and Goody Soda. It is conceivable that Twin Lights might carry on by eventually licensing out the name in such a fashion. Otherwise, there is nobody left after Pierce to do it.

"I've had lots of people approach us wanting to do something. There are people who want the name now, to do something on their own somewhere else, asking to license or buy the name. Some have ideas about things like, oh, flavored water," he laughs. "I've also had guys on the phone from some of the bigger companies. In recent years, they seem to be calling from further and further afar."

Pierce does not want to give up the name just yet, but neither can he envision doing anything drastically different with the business than he is doing now. "You know," he pauses for a moment, "it's just not modern enough. The machinery is not modern enough, I am not modern enough. I do not do my bookkeeping on a computer. We do not even do credit cards—that stuff is all alien to me. Apparently, I am on Facebook now, but I do not even know how that works. I have a nice little niche, so I don't see any point in upsetting the apple cart."

But he also admits that he is not sure how much longer he can even keep it going as a niche enterprise. Pierce ordered his last three one-gallon containers of the number fourteen ginger ale extract from Foote & Jenks in 2017, after finding out that they were about to stop making it. ("I usually ordered two at a time," he says. "But I bought an extra when I found out it was the end of it.") He is hoping it will be enough to last. He insists it is. But you simply cannot make Twin Lights' signature Pale Dry Ginger Ale without it.

"It's OK, what I have left should be enough," he says, not entirely reassuring. He is not interested in trying to formulate a new version, either. "It doesn't matter now, because the machine is old, I'm old, everything is declining and the only places where we sell now are when people come to get it, or I deliver it."

On paper, that probably sounds like resignation. But to hear Pierce speak, it sounds more like pragmatism and satisfaction. "I feel really lucky," he insists. "I've been able to run Twin Lights for twenty-five years, and I was lucky that I had a guy that could fix the machines and a guy that could help me find bottles."

In fact, when his father George Sears died, his mother told him it would be OK if he did not want to keep the business going. Heck, Pierce had already hit retirement age by that point. "But I couldn't just let it end," he says. "Not at that time. But now, I think I'm OK with just letting us kind of slowly fade out."

He could not just sell the business, either. For one thing, it sits right on his property. To reach the plant from the house, you walk across the driveway to the side yard, so there is not enough space to turn things over to other people. Even trickier, Twin Lights is grandfathered under current zoning laws. If the company changed hands, the town could void that permission. Then there's the board of health. Years ago, Twin Lights employees used to chuckle when the health inspector showed up and put on a hard hat before walking into the garage to look at their tiny operation. But, in recent years, it had started to become more of a nuisance. "Last time the health inspector came up from Boston to pay a visit, I had only two or three retail outlets left," Pierce explains. "The health department guy said, 'Well, if you give up the retail and stick to private deliveries, I do not have to bother you anymore. But otherwise, you'd stay under our jurisdiction.' So that was when I decided to give up on retail entirely."

As a historian and now longtime resident, I believe that the townspeople of Rockport treasure Twin Lights Tonic more than Pierce realizes. "He is truly unique. He will deliver the order to you personally, he is committed to staying with the old, returnable bottles. Twin Lights is a little bit of Americana that, without people like Pierce Sears, would be only a distant memory."

As for the lucky number fourteen ginger ale extract, Pierce concedes that there is actually very little left. "It's a small amount," he admits. "Less than half a gallon. I would say I have enough for another ten to twenty cases and then once that is gone, well…I think Twin Lights will be gone, too."

"But, you know, I can't believe how well we did. And considering where we are located—all the way up here at the end of the line, surrounded on three sides by water, in this relatively small area…I'm perfectly happy with that."

BIBLIOGRAPHY

Books and Periodicals

American Carbonator and Bottler.

Breaking Down the Chain: A Guide to the Soft Drink Industry. Oakland, CA: Change Lab Solutions, 2018.

Donovan, Tristan. *Fizz: How Soda Shook Up the World.* Chicago: Chicago Review Press, 2013.

Grand View Research. *Carbonated Soft Drinks Market Size, Share & Trends Analysis Report by Distribution Channel, Competitive Landscape, by Region, and Segment Forecasts, 2018–2025.* San Francisco, 2018.

Hill, Benjamin D. *The North Shore of Massachusetts Bay: An Illustrated Guide to Marblehead, Salem, Peabody, Beverly, Manchester-by-the-Sea, Magnolia, Gloucester, Rockport, and Ipswich.* Salem, MA: Salem Press, 1881.

Jacobsen, Jessica. "2018 Soft Drink Report: Carbonated Soft Drink Manufacturers Adapt to Formulation, Engagement Trends." *Beverage Industry Magazine* (April 2018).

Morrison, Sara. "Chelmsford Is All About Its Golden Ginger Ale." *Boston Magazine* (September 2014).

National Bottlers' Gazette.

Riley, John J., *Organization in the Soft Drink Industry: A History of the American Bottlers of Carbonated Beverages.* N.p.: American Bottlers of Carbonated Beverages, 1946.

Sulz, Charles Herman. *A Treatise on Beverages, Or the Complete Practical Bottler.* New York: Dick & Fitzgerald, 1888.

Tufts, James W. *The Manufacture and Bottling of Carbonated Beverages.* N.p., 1887.

Collections

Cape Ann Museum, Gloucester, Massachusetts, photo collection and website.

Library of Congress Digital Photo Archives.

Sandy Bay Historical Society, Rockport, Massachusetts, Glass Plate Negative Collection.

Online Sources

Antique Bottles. www.antiquebottles.com.

Family Search. www.familysearch.com.

Hutchbook. www.hutchbook.com.

Pop vs Soda. www.popvssoda.com.

Vintage Rockport. www.vintagerockport.com.

ACKNOWLEDGEMENTS

Special thanks to: William Comstock, Harvard University Libraries; the Sawyer Free Library, Gloucester, Massachusetts; Rockport Public Library, Rockport, Massachusetts; Thacher Island Association, Rockport, Massachusetts; Sandy Bay Historical Society, Rockport, Massachusetts; John Salisbury; Abby Battis, Beverly Historical Society; Christopher Weide, Platform 3 Research; Bob Ambrogi, vintagerockport.com; Earl and Nancy Fitzgerald; Susan and Phillip Elliot Hopkins; Joel Kenniston; Anders Johnson; Chester Clark; Eddie Everett; and Pierce Sears.

INDEX

V

W

ABOUT THE AUTHORS

Paul St. Germain has been a resident of Rockport, Massachusetts, for the past twenty-five years. His interest in Cape Ann area began in 1999, when he was asked to join the Thacher Island Association's Board of Directors eventually elected president in 2002. In 2000, he researched and wrote the successful nomination application resulting in the designation of the Cape Ann Light Station on Thacher Island as a National Historic Landmark by the Interior Department's National Park Service. He has written four books in Arcadia Publishing's Images of America series: *Sandy Bay Harbor of Refuge and the Navy*, *Cape Ann Granite*, *Lighthouses and Lifesaving Stations on Cape Ann* and *Twin Lights of Thacher Island*. Most recently, he has written a fifth book for The History Press: *Saving Straitsmouth Island: A History.*

A graduate of Boston University and a master's degree recipient from Northeastern University, he has held several senior-level marketing and advertising positions of major international athletic footwear and soft drink manufacturers.

Devlin Sherlock is a writer, broadcaster and curator. He is also a New England native and one-time resident of Rockport. His writing has appeared in over a dozen publications, including *Rolling Stone*, *Billboard*, *Womens Health* and *Surfer Magazine*, while he was featured on such broadcast outlets as NPR and the BBC (UK). His career began on Cape Ann, working at the *Musician Magazine* offices in Gloucester is his first "real" job. He is currently music festival programmer for South by Southwest (SXSW), the global music, film and technology conference in Austin, Texas.